A Parent's Guide™ to
Seattle

POST ALLEY

parent's guide press
Los Angeles, CA
www.pgpress.com

A Parent's Guide™ to
Seattle

Text and Maps © Mars Publishing 2002

Cover design by Michael Duggan
  Cover photos by Nick Gunderson (Public Market Center, Space Needle)
  Cover photos by Andrea Einig-Homann (Seattle Skyline, Japanese Garden, Seattle Downtown)

Interior Photos © Photographers as noted

ISBN: 1-931199-10-8

Mars Publishing and the Mars Publishing Logo, Parent's Guide and the Parent's Guide logo are trademarks of Mars Publishing, Inc. The author and Mars Publishing have tried to make the information in this book as accurate as possible. We accept no responsibility for any loss, injury, or inconvenience sustained by anyone using this book.

This book, and all titles in the Parent's Guide series, are available for purposes of fund raising and educational sales to charity drives, fund raisers, parent or teacher organizations, schools, government agencies and corporations at a discount for purchases of more than 10 copies. Persons or organizations wishing to inquire should call Mars Publishing at 1-800-549-6646 or write to us at *sales@marspub.com*.

At the time of publication of this book, all of the information contained within was correct to the best of our knowledge. If you find information in this book that has changed, please contact us. Even better, if you have additional places to recommend, please let us know. Any included submissions to the new edition of this book will get the submitter a by-line in the book and a free copy of any Mars publication.

Please contact us at *parentsguides@marspub.com*

parent's guide press

Edwin E. Steussy, CEO and Publisher
Lars Y. Peterson, Project Editor
Michael P. Duggan, Graphic Artist

PO Box 461730
Los Angeles CA 90046

contents

Dedication

Following several years in Europe, my wife and I returned to Seattle, only to discover parenthood and with it a whole new perspective on this wonderful city. I dedicate this book to my wife, Jennifer, daughter, Josephine, to two sets of loving grandparents, and to all those members of our extended-family with whom we take great pleasure in sharing Seattle.

Tom Hobson

Introduction

When I worked for the Greater Seattle Chamber of Commerce during the 1980s, locals complained the Californians were taking over, trying to change the fundamental nature of Seattle. It was fun to have outsiders to castigate for problems of congestion and overbuilding, but our blame was misplaced. The chamber's research manager once told me that the number of "outsiders" moving here was pretty much on par with other American cities. The factor that caused the alarming growth rate was that young people weren't moving away like they did from other cities. People who grew up here wanted to stay.

This phenomenon has a long history in Seattle. During the mid-1960s, when the so-called "Boeing Bust" caused the aerospace giant to layoff some 60,000 workers, a prankster put up a now-famous billboard reading, "Will the last person leaving Seattle please turn out the lights?" Some did leave, but a majority of these highly trained technical workers and engineers stayed, providing a foundation for the technology sector that was to emerge a decade later – lead by Microsoft – and is still booming today.

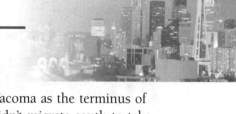

Introduction

In 1874, when the Northern Pacific railroad selected Tacoma as the terminus of its transcontinental railroad instead of Seattle, residents didn't migrate south to take part in the anticipated economic boom, but rather remained in Seattle, where hundreds of citizens from all walks of life went to work building our own railroad along the Duwamish River.

I've been a Seattle lover since visiting with my family as a 14-year-old. Freshly minted bachelor's degree in hand, I moved here in 1984, where I met and married my wife Jennifer. We've lived in other parts of the U.S. and even in Europe, but when we decided to start a family, we both knew that Seattle was where we wanted to be.

When I tell people I'm from Seattle, they invariably say something like "I've heard it's beautiful, but how do you stand the rain?"

So ingrained is this impression that I don't even bother explaining that the Emerald City has less annual rainfall than New York, Atlanta, or Boston. Instead, I point out that it's the precipitation that makes for the green forests, the snowcapped mountains and the sparkling bodies of water. Unlike elsewhere, people don't run for the hills when it turns hot, but stay right in the city to enjoy the most spectacular summer weather imaginable. I point out that most of the moisture that falls from the sky is of the misty rather than torrential variety – what I call "walking rain" (because it's a refreshing rather than a soaking dampness) or what our daughter, Josephine, calls "faint rain" (because you can't even hear it falling).

What looks to others like perpetual rain for nine months of the year is really a stubborn cloud cover that moves in around mid-October and doesn't vacate the sky until the ides of May. Where others might be depressed by the gloom and damp, Seattleites learn to find the soft, natural beauty that can only exist in such a place; to glory in those unexpected days when clouds vanish, leaving the world sparkling and colorful like no other place on earth; to be introspective over a mug of coffee and a good book; to entertain a deep, moody creativity that finds vent in a vibrant underground of eclectic art and music. More than anything else, it's this weather that dictates the casual democracy of fashion one finds here – where men hide their business suits under parkas and women wear boots instead of high heels; where corporate executives stand side-by-side with street people, all wearing the same sloppy rain hats, while waiting for the crosswalk light to change; where the sale of sunglasses is among the highest in the world because we lose them between sun breaks.

Introduction

If you stay off of the roads during rush hour, you'll likely come to think of Seattleites as polite, although perhaps not overly sociable. People with varying lifestyles, beliefs, ethnicities, and political ideologies live together with relative ease in our city, a situation made possible, at least in part, by a prevailing ethic of "tending ones' own garden," which may strike newcomers as unfriendly. It's a remnant of the not too distant days of pioneers, who moved west for the express purpose of finding the room to live in freedom as each individual saw fit. Perhaps more than anything else, it is this individuality that defines Seattle.

This is the Seattle I grew to love, but since the birth of our daughter, Josephine, a new city has been opened to me over the past 5 years – a place for families. This is the city I hope to introduce to you in this book.

How to Use This Book

The rest of this chapter will deal with the things you need to know in order for you to get the most out of your visit to Seattle. A brief history of the area is followed by a section on Seattle as you will find it today: its people, economy, arts, and seasons. You will also find information about our climate and a general geographic orientation. There are several options for getting around the Seattle area, and these are profiled here as well. An overview of the local media has also been included, as well as a short directory of tourist and emergency contact information, a listing of "bus" tour operators, a tip for saving money on major attractions, and a word about Seattle's family-oriented community centers.

Chapters Two, Three, and Four are a district-by-district, neighborhood-by-neighborhood listing of things to do, eat, and buy with your children. As Seattle is truly a city of neighborhoods and a great place to walk about, our method is to provide driving directions to the various areas of interest and then to presume you will spend some time getting to know the place, getting around on foot from attraction to attraction. We've provided more detailed directions for neighborhoods that are too spread out for walking. Our focus has been on the things that make Seattle special, which is why you won't find a great deal of information about national chains or shopping malls like those one can find anywhere. Every effort has been made to include costs, hours, and other details, but things change, so make sure to phone first.

Chapter Five takes you outside of the Seattle city limits on outings to the north, south, east, and west.

Finally, you will find a calendar of annual events.

Introduction

A Brief History of Seattle

Early Explorers

In May of 1792, Captain George Vancouver (1757-98) and his men aboard the warship *Discovery* became the first "white men" to enter Puget Sound. They made a quick survey of the land, named several of the most obvious landmarks and islands, then little more than a week later, continued northward in search of the illusive "Northwest Passage" which they believed linked the Atlantic and Pacific Oceans.

Legend has it that the young brave who was to become Chief Seattle was among those native Americans who witnessed Vancouver's arrival upon Puget Sound waters.

Eleven years later, President Thomas Jefferson (1743-1826) doubled the area of the United States when he made the "Louisiana Purchase" from France. In 1804, Meriwether Lewis (1774-1809) and Captain William Clark (1770-1838) set out on their famed westward expedition to explore this newly acquired land. Although the expedition made it to the Pacific Ocean and spent some 8 months in the area that comprises the southern parts of what is now Washington State, neither they or any other of the 33 person contingent made their way as far north as the Puget Sound region. They, like Vancouver before them, were more interested in discovering a water passage. This one, they hoped, would be cross-continental, linking the east and west coasts of North America via the Mississippi and Columbia Rivers.

Great Britain and the United States

Although Jefferson had paid for the land, Great Britain and the United States continued to squabble over the Pacific Northwest. In 1818, as part of the peacemaking process that followed the War of 1812, the two nations signed a treaty. They agreed, essentially, to *share* what was then known as the Oregon Territory, an untenable situation at best.

In 1841, American Captain Charles Wilkes (1798-1877) and his crew entered the Puget Sound on a surveying expedition, marking the first official American entry into the region. Wilkes, like Vancouver and Lewis and Clark before him, was not all that impressed by what he named "Elliott Bay" (in honor of one of the three Elliotts in his crew – which one, no one knows for sure), saying that it was not a "desirable anchorage." (Incidentally, Wilkes' severe and arrogant style of command is said to have been the model for Herman Melville's most magnificent of American literary figures, Captain Ahab, from the novel *Moby Dick*.)

Introduction

In 1843, the American settlers formed their own government and for a period of three years existed as an independent nation. But in 1846, Britain gave up its claim to the Oregon Territory, leaving it in the hands of the U.S.

The final area of dispute between the two nations was what to do about the San Juan Islands, situated in the northern reaches of Puget Sound. Both countries fortified the islands, claiming sovereignty. The pot nearly bubbled over in 1858, when an American killed a British pig he found in his potato patch. War was, in fact, narrowly avoided, although the incident has come to be known to posterity as the "San Juan Pig War."

First Settlers

The area's earliest settlers were scattered about the region, most notably south of Seattle. The local Indian tribes (primarily Duwamish, Snolqualmie, Chehalis, Nisqually, and Snohomish) were for the most part opposed to these white encroachers and sought to drive them out wherever possible.

When Arthur Denny and his party of settlers from the Midwest arrived in the area in 1851, they first settled at Alki Point (a pylon at Alki Beach marks the "landing" today), which is situated in what we now call West Seattle, across Elliott Bay from downtown. It is known that they met Chief Seattle, and while he may not have been exactly welcoming, he didn't try to drive them away either. By 1852, the Denny party had moved across the bay to what is today Pioneer Square.

Comprising this first group of Seattleites were 10 adults and 12 children. (Okay, okay, the settlement was actually called "Duwamps" at the time, so they were technically "Duwampites." By the time the first post office was opened later that year, however, the name "Seattle" was official.)

It might have taken awhile for European settlers to fully appreciate the potential of the area, but even before they were established, economic and population growth erupted, making 1852 one of the most important years in early Seattle's history.

Another important settler arrived that fall – Henry Yesler (1810-92). He was seeking a place to build a steam-powered lumber mill. The ideal site would require lots of timber and easy water access, both of which he found on the shores of Elliott Bay. He would also need workers, a resource not nearly as plentiful when it came to Europeans, but easily solved by his being the first white settler to employ Native Americans. By early 1853, the mill was up and running: Seattle's first industrial enterprise. Most of the lumber was sent to San Francisco to help rebuild after their great fire, but enough stayed behind to build 20 buildings, mostly in and around what is now Pioneer Square.

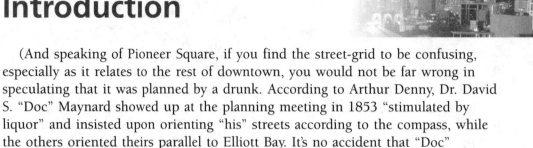

Introduction

(And speaking of Pioneer Square, if you find the street-grid to be confusing, especially as it relates to the rest of downtown, you would not be far wrong in speculating that it was planned by a drunk. According to Arthur Denny, Dr. David S. "Doc" Maynard showed up at the planning meeting in 1853 "stimulated by liquor" and insisted upon orienting "his" streets according to the compass, while the others oriented theirs parallel to Elliott Bay. It's no accident that "Doc" Maynard's remains one of Pioneer Square's most venerable bars, although it is emphatically *not* a place to go with children.)

The Great Fire

By the 1880s, Pioneer Square had become a true downtown, with retailers, banks, an assortment of service providers, and a burgeoning cultural community.

In a matter of hours on June 6, 1889, an upset pot of glue became the flash-point for a fire that consumed the wooden buildings covering a 30-block area: a conflagration that came to be known as the Great Fire of 1889. No human lives were lost, but the devastation was complete.

Not to be defeated, however, the city was quickly rebuilt, this time of stone and brick, although you will only see what's left of these buildings today by taking the Underground Tour (of which you will read later in this book).

The Klondike Gold Rush

One of the most significant events in the history of Seattle was the Klondike Gold Rush, which began in 1897 when a steamship arrived in Seattle with a ship-ment of nearly 2 tons of gold from Alaska's Yukon River.

As the most advantageous place from which to launch gold mining expeditions into Alaska, Seattle became the staging area for thousands upon thousands of hopeful prospectors seeking their fortunes. Providing supplies, equipment, banks and "services" (such as saloons and brothels), the city enjoyed economic boom times that culminated in 1914 with the construction of the 42-story Smith Tower, which at 522 feet remained the tallest building in the U.S. outside of New York until after World War II.

Introduction

World War II and the 1962 World's Fair

Along with the rest of the nation, Seattle suffered through the Great Depression in the 1930s, then enjoyed the economic rebirth associated with World War II. The local economy rode through the 1950s on the shoulders of the Boeing Company and in 1962, Seattle, brimming with confidence, hosted the World's Fair. The fair was a success by any measure, leaving behind the most enduring modern symbol of Seattle – the Space Needle – as well as a sense of confidence and destiny that influences the city's collective consciousness to this day.

Seattle Today

Today's Seattle is a vibrant, international city of commerce, culture, and community that still rotates around its vital downtown.

The People

The Greater Seattle area – which includes King, Pierce, and Island counties – has a population of nearly 2.5 million people, 560,000 (give or take) of whom live within the Seattle city limits. Seattle is home to an educated population with nearly 40 percent holding at least a bachelor's degree, and a diverse population, with its non-white population approaching 30 percent. Nearly 15 percent of Seattle's residents speak a language other than English at home.

Introduction

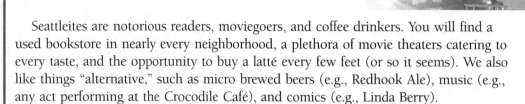

Seattleites are notorious readers, moviegoers, and coffee drinkers. You will find a used bookstore in nearly every neighborhood, a plethora of movie theaters catering to every taste, and the opportunity to buy a latté every few feet (or so it seems). We also like things "alternative," such as micro brewed beers (e.g., Redhook Ale), music (e.g., any act performing at the Crocodile Café), and comics (e.g., Linda Berry).

The Environment

Nicknamed the "Emerald City" because it's so "green," Seattle may be home to the most wildlife of any major city in the U.S. Forget the pigeons, squirrels, and rats that constitute "wildlife" in other cities. Bald eagles, peregrine falcons, salmon, sea lions, Orca whales, octopi, raccoons, mountain beaver, seagulls, bats, and even coyotes (some 50 are believed to live *in* Seattle) reside here, at least on a seasonal basis. With over 5,000 acres of parks, dozens of lakes, and Puget Sound as our doorstep, Seattle is one of the least urbanized cities in the nation.

The Politics

Politically, Seattle tends to vote Democrat, while the suburbs tend to go Republican. Our history of political activism runs deep, with literally hundreds, if not thousands, of committees, organizations, and community action groups active in the Puget Sound region. The environment is probably the cause with the most popular support. For the most part, our region's governments are considered "clean," albeit, at times ineffective and bumbling. The business community exerts a strong influence in local politics.

The Economics

Despite an increase in economic diversity during the past couple of decades, aerospace giant Boeing remains the region's largest employer. Microsoft, the Port of Seattle, Alaska Air, and the University of Washington are more or less bunched up in a "dead heat" in second place. More than half of us work in the wholesale, retail, and services sector of the economy, with manufacturing jobs amounting to about 15 percent of the total workforce and government jobs providing 13 percent. King County's median annual household income is close to $60,000, although people in the suburbs tend to earn nearly twice that of a Seattle resident.

Introduction

The Arts

Although Seattle's music scene (don't let anyone hear you use the word "grunge") was the most recent segment of the local arts community to attract national attention, there is a lot more here than loud guitars. For one thing, you can't turn around without finding yourself face-to-face with some piece of public art. The new Seattle Art Museum is popular with locals and visitors alike. Seattle is becoming known as a dance center with its nationally acclaimed Pacific Northwest Ballet. Having spawned such homegrown modern dance talent as Mark Morris, Trisha Brown, and Robert Joffrey helped, too. Outside of New York, Seattle is arguably the most theater-going city in the U.S. Beyond rock music, Seattle venues offer world-class jazz, blues and world music, not to mention the Seattle Opera and Symphony, and the new Experience Music Project.

Facts and Figures

The Weather

Temperatures in Seattle rarely get below freezing, nor over about 75 degrees, although an hour's drive eastward during the winter will bring you into the winter wonderland of the Cascade Mountains, and 3 hours in the same direction during the summer will land you in the eastern part of Washington state where temperatures regularly reach the mid-90s. When we do experience a heat wave, work stops as everyone stampedes for the boats and beaches. This is followed, if the heat doesn't break, by the most pathetic suffering you'll see anywhere – it doesn't help that the vast majority of homes don't have air conditioning. Every few years, we get enough snow that it sticks, causing general panic amongst the population. Once more, work stops as most Seattleites leave their cars in the garage and stay home. Those that attempt to drive promptly slam their vehicles into one another.

You will want to pack raingear if you intend to visit from about mid-October through mid-April, which is the rainy season, although you can't really count on sunny weather until mid-June. A typical non-summer Seattle day is cool, drizzly, and overcast (we average some 200 cloudy days annually and nearly 100 more that are defined as partly cloudy). Summer days tend to start off foggy or hazy, then become mild and sunny, a trend that often lasts through September.

Introduction

Geography

The shape of Seattle is long and lean, pinched at the waist – wasp like – by the saltwater of Elliott Bay to the west and the freshwater of Lake Washington to the east. Seattle is spread over a hilly terrain, dotted by lakes and intersected by waterways, both natural and manmade. We are surrounded by mountains, the best-known of which is Mt. Rainier, a geographic feature that, when the "mountain is out," makes even a drive down junky Rainier Ave. S into a breathtaking experience. The snow-topped Olympic Mountains tower over Seattle's skyline as drivers head west on I-90. The Cascade Mountains rising to the east provide easy access to fantastic wintertime recreation.

The area across Lake Washington is known as "the Eastside," which includes the cities of Bellevue, Kirkland, Redmond, and a number of smaller communities. Long considered mere suburbs, they have in the past couple of decades emerged as major cities in their own right.

As Seattle sprawls northward along Interstate 5, you pass through a number of suburban communities and cross into Snohomish County before coming to Everett, home of the famous Boeing factory tour.

The southward sprawl carries you to Tacoma, the state's second largest city.

Getting Around Seattle

I wish I could recommend easy, inexpensive mass transit options, but they don't exist. Your primary options – after a car – are taxis (which get very expensive, very fast) or Metro buses, which are fantastic for commuters, but can be quite confusing and time consuming for many visitors, who generally need more flexibility than bus schedules allow. I'm not saying you can't traverse Seattle by bus, just that you'll need to do some planning in order to make it work.

Personally, I find cycling to be a great way to get around, but that usually means getting out into traffic, so I don't do it with our daughter, Josephine.

Driving In and Around Seattle

The Seattle-area is annually ranked as one of the most traffic congested areas in the country.

Generally speaking, it's relatively easy to travel north and south in the Seattle area – it's east and west that kill you. The major north-south routes are I-5

Introduction

(through the heart of Seattle – most of the directions given in this book use I-5 as the starting point), I-405 (through the Eastside), and State Route 99/Aurora (skirting the western edge of the city), but there are a number of other options for savvy drivers only needing to cover a portion of the north-south distance.

Seattle is connected to the Eastside by a pair of bridges: the so-called 520 bridge (Evergreen Point Floating Bridge) to the north and the I-90 bridge (Mercer Island Floating Bridge) to the south. Traffic tends to travel faster on the newer, wider I-90 bridge, but keep in mind that Eastside traffic is often worse than Seattle's. If your destination is significantly closer to 520, take that bridge even if things are sluggish. Incidentally, these bridges are an engineering solution worth seeing – the 520 bridge is even a drawbridge that opens sideways!

Safety seats are required by law for all children under 40 lbs. And starting July 1, 2002, car seats or booster seats will be required until a child is 60 lbs. or 6 years old. Experts, however, recommend use of booster seats until 80 lbs. and 57 inches tall, or until the vehicle seatbelts alone will fit. This puts most children in booster seats until age 8 or older.

Driving Tips:

- I go to extremes to avoid driving during the morning and afternoon commutes. If possible, stay off Interstate 5 during those hours.

- Martin Luther King Jr. Way is an underutilized route connecting the Madison Valley/Madison Park area in the north to the southern-most reaches of Seattle.

- Lake Washington Blvd./Lakeside Ave. S offers a beautiful drive along Lake Washington connecting Madison Park in the north to Seward Park in the south. Although your speed is limited to 25 mph, the route is rarely congested, and there are very few stop signs along the gently winding route. Don't let the lake and mountain vistas distract you. Watch out for cyclists.

- Airport Way South is another under-utilized route, connecting downtown with Seattle's south-end. It more or less parallels I-5.

- State Route 99/Aurora runs from the northern city limit to the southern. Of the major north-south routes, it tends to be the lesser of three evils. The best Elliott Bay views in the city are from the top deck (heading north) of the viaduct that separates downtown from the waterfront.

- Contributing greatly to Seattle's traffic problems is the fact that it is a city divided by water. Lake Union, Lake Washington Ship Canal, Portage Bay, and Union Bay combine to split the city's northern and southern parts. This means that crossing from one to the other requires choosing a bridge, all of which are drawbridges with the exceptions of the Freeway Bridge (I-5) and the Aurora Avenue Bridge (SR 99). Generally speaking, the Aurora Bridge is the most reliable option.

- Lake City Way angles northeastward from about Green Lake to the city limit and, even with its numerous stoplights, is often more efficient than other routes.

Introduction

- Traveling east-west in north Seattle is one of the most frustrating driving experiences in the city. Avoid 45th St. if you are in a hurry. I tend to favor NE 75th St. when traveling east-west on the east side of I-5 and N/NW 85th St. when west of I-5.

- East-West travel in the south-end is frustrated less by traffic volume and more by the fact that so many of the streets are interrupted by I-5. I tend to favor E Yesler Way, S McClellan St., and S Myrtle/Othello.

- When traveling on the Interstate highways, keep an eye out for faster-moving, high-occupancy vehicle lanes (designated by a diamond shape). In most cases, this means that only vehicles with two or more occupants are permitted (although there are some stretches that require three). One of the goals of these lanes is to encourage carpooling, but the way the law is written, even a child under driving age counts toward a carpool. Take advantage!

- If you plan to head into the mountains anytime other than during the summer, be prepared with snow chains or tires, which are often required. For highway information, call 1-800-695-ROAD or within Seattle (206) 368-4499.

Taking the Bus

Taking the bus in Seattle requires planning. You can pick up schedules on buses and at libraries, major shopping malls, government offices, and other places, but it's easiest to just grab a pencil and call Metro's 24-hour hotline: (206) 553-3000. Tell them where you are, where you're going, and what time you want to leave or arrive, and they'll tell you where to wait and when, including transfer information. They will also provide fare information or mail you a timetable if you ask. For bus passes, phone: (206) 624-PASS. Metro's website is also very helpful: **http://transit.metrokc.gov**.

You might be interested in Metro's Park & Ride lots, which allow you to park for free and travel by bus. These lots, however, are generally very popular and fill up early. Call the hotline for more information.

Our favorite aspect of Metro's system is the ride-free zone, between 6 a.m. and 7 p.m., in downtown. The zone is encompassed by Jackson St. to the south, Battery St. on the north, 6th Ave. on the east, and the waterfront to the west (excluding the Waterfront Trolley). You can hop on any bus heading any direction within this zone and ride for free. This is a great way to cover ground quickly and cheaply. If you're worried about accidentally traveling beyond the ride-free borders, make sure to ask the driver to announce his/her last stop within the zone.

Introduction

Metro claims to offer one of the safest bus systems in the U.S. and I personally have never felt threatened on a bus, although I've never traveled late at night when problems tend to occur. If you are on a bus between 9 p.m. and 5 a.m., you can ask the driver to stop anywhere along the route, and – depending on his/her assessment of the safety of your request – you'll be let off there.

All Metro buses are wheelchair accessible, permit dogs (as long as they don't take up a seat), and have bike racks on the front.

Taxis

You might get lucky, but unless you're downtown, the only way to get a taxi is to call. By far the cleanest, most reliable taxi company is Orange Cab (206) 522-8800.

If you are downtown and don't have access to a phone, you can usually find taxis waiting outside the big hotels.

Bicycling

If you can get there by car, you can get there by bike, assuming, of course, you have the time and stamina.

King County is one of the best urban areas in the U.S. for cycling. If your family plans to spend a lot of time in the saddle (and I only recommend this if your children are at least teenagers with good cycling skills), log-on to **www.metrokc.gov/kcdot/tp/bike/bikemap.htm** or call (206) 263-4729 or (206) 263-4788 and order a free copy of the King County Department of Transportation's comprehensive bicycling guide map. The map not only details the hundreds of miles of bike accessible trails, paths, and lanes throughout the county, but also provides valuable information about state and county laws, safety tips, and how to use the bike racks on Metro busses.

Even if helmets were not required by law, it would be foolish for you or your child to set off without one. Head injuries are the most common bicycle-related injury, causing about 1,000 deaths and more than 400,000 hospital visits in the U.S. each year.

Introduction

Local Media

Major daily newspapers

Seattle Post-Intelligencer
Seattle Times
Eastside Journal

Major weeklies

Seattle Weekly
The Stranger

Local family-oriented publication

Seattle's Child (available for free at many child-oriented venues – **www.parenthood.com** or call (206) 441-0191)

Television

KOMO-TV (Channel 4) – ABC affiliate
KING-TV (Channel 5) – NBC affiliate
KONG-TV (Channel 6) – KING-TV sister station
KIRO-TV (Channel 7) – CBS affiliate
KCTS-TV (Channel 9) – PBS affiliate
KSTW-TV (Channel 11) – UPN affiliate
KCPQ-TV (Channel 13) – Fox affiliate
KTZZ-TV (Channel 22) – WB affiliate

Introduction

Selected radio stations

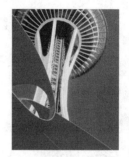

KISW (100-FM) – Album-oriented rock
KZOK (102.5-FM) – Classic rock
KNDD (107.7-FM) – Alternative rock
KBSG (1210-AM, 97.3-FM) – Oldies
KUBE (93.3-FM) – Contemporary hits
KIRO (710-AM) – News, talk, sports, info.
KJR (950-AM) – Sports
KUOW (94.9-AM) – National Public Radio
KOMO-AM (1000-AM) News, talk, sports, info. ("Pat Cashman Show" on
   weekday mornings is one of those rare birds that is both "clean" and hilarious.)
KPLU (88.5-FM) – Jazz, National Public Radio
KING (98.1-FM) – Classical
KMPS (1300-AM, 94.1-FM) – Country

Phone Numbers You Should Have

Ambulance/fire/emergency	911
Greater Seattle Chamber of Commerce	(206) 389-7200
Highway information	1-800-695-ROAD
Metro (bus) information	(206) 553-3000
Seattle-King Co. Visitors and Convention Bureau	(206) 461-5840
Seattle Poison Center	(206) 526-2121 or 1-800-732-6985
Seattle-Tacoma International Airport info.	(206) 431-4444
Wading Pool Hotline (check to see if pools are open)	(206) 684-7796
Washington State Ferries	(206) 464-6400

Introduction

"Bus" Tours

Ride the Ducks of Seattle

516 Broad St.
(206) 441-3825

A unique, silly city tour on land and water aboard vintage WWII amphibious vehicles.

Gray Line City Sights Bus Tour

720 S Forest St.
(206) 624-5813

At 3 hours, this traditional city tour is too long for small children.

Seattle Trolley Tours

(206) 626-5208

Tacoma Narrows Bridge

Operating from mid-May through Mid-October, these "trolleys" (buses dolled up to look like trolleys) make 11 stops at major tourist spots around the city. Look for "sandwich" boards designating stops or call.

Save Money

If you intend to visit several of the city's popular attractions, we advise you to consider the purchase of a CityPass, which for $33.50 gains you admission to: the Woodland Park Zoo, Space Needle, Pacific Science Center, Seattle Aquarium, Argosy Cruises Harbor Tour *and* the Museum of Flight. That's about half-price. You can purchase a CityPass at any of these venues or on-line at **www.citypass.com**.

Introduction

Community Centers/Indoor Playgrounds

Seattle's Parks and Recreation Department operates 24 community centers in the city. These facilities offer a variety of programs and classes of interest to families at a nominal cost, including, in most cases, "indoor playgrounds" for toddlers. Given the Pacific Northwest's propensity for rain, this is something we feel that families of young children ought to know about. We've written in more detail about a handful of these facilities later in this book. More information can be had by calling the numbers listed below or checking the community center website at **www.cityofseattle.net/parks/Centers/index.htm**.

Alki Community Center
5817 SW Stevens
(206) 684-7430

Ballard Community Center
6020 28th Ave. NW
(206) 684-4093

Bitter Lake Community Center
13035 Linden Ave. N
(206) 684-7524

Delridge Community Center
4501 Delridge Way SW
(206) 684-7423

Garfield Community Center
2323 East Cherry
(206) 684-4788

Green Lake Community Center
7201 E Green Lake Dr. N
(206) 684-0780

Hiawatha Community Center
2700 California Ave. SW
(206) 684-7441

Introduction

High Point Community Center
6920 34th Ave. SW
(206) 684-7422

Jefferson Community Center
3801 Beacon Ave. S
(206) 684-7481

Laurelhurst Community Center
4554 NE 41st St.
(206) 684-7529

Langston Hughes Cultural Arts Center
104 17th Ave. S
(206) 684-4757

Loyal Heights Community Center
2101 NW 77th St.
(206) 684-4052

Magnolia Community Center
2550 34th Ave. W
(206) 386-4235

Meadowbrook Community Center
10517 35th Ave. NE
(206) 684-7522

Miller Community Center
330-19th Ave. E
(206) 684-4753

Montlake Community Center
1618 E Calhoun St.
(206) 684-4736

Queen Anne Community Center
1901 First Ave. W
(206) 386-4240

Rainier Community Center
4600 28th Ave. S
(206) 386-1919

Rainier Beach Community Center
8825 Rainier Ave. S
(206) 386-1925

Ravenna-Eckstein Community Center
6535 Ravenna NE
(206) 684-7534

South Park Community Center
8319 Eighth Ave. S
(206) 684-7451

Southwest Community Center
2801 SW Thistle St.
(206) 684-7438

Van Asselt Community Center
2820 S Myrtle St.
(206) 386-1921

Yesler Community Center
835 E Yesler Way
(206) 386-1245

1 Downtown

Our daughter's first home was on the corner of First Avenue and Virginia Street, one block up from the Pike Place Market. Our kitchen window framed the Space Needle. From our bedroom she saw Lake Union. The living room provided an awe-inspiring vista that featured the mouth of the Duwamish lined with the bright red Port of Seattle cranes and Mt. Rainier as a backdrop. The dining room sparkled with the reflected light of Elliott Bay.

Downtown is hemmed-in by Elliott Bay to the west, I-5 to the east, Seattle Center to the north, and what is called the Sodo district to the south. Orienting yourself is as easy as spotting the water or the Space Needle. In spite of the hills, downtown is a fantastic place for pedestrians, and a reasonably fit adult, or an older child, can easily walk anywhere within these boundaries. You will want a stroller for younger children.

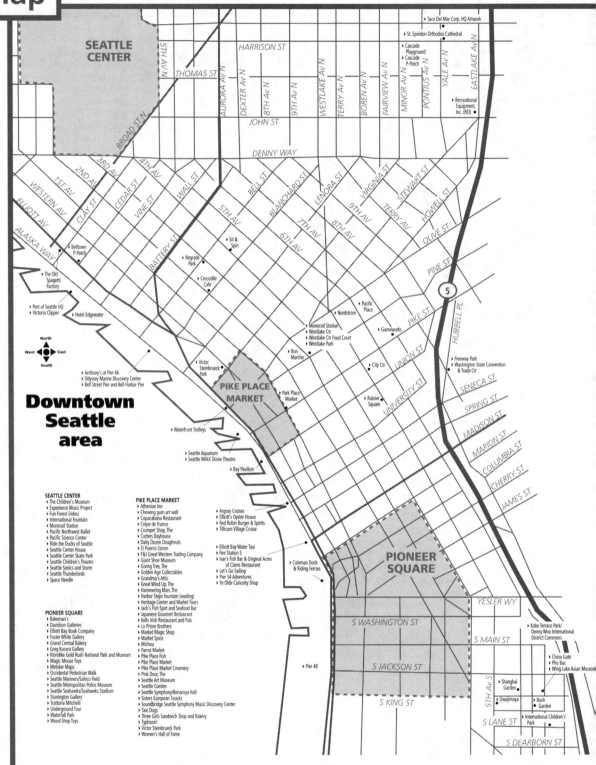

map

SEATTLE CENTER

Downtown Seattle area

North
West · East
South

Taco Del Mar Corp. HQ Artwork
St. Spiridon Orthodox Cathedral
Cascade Playground
Cascade P-Patch
Recreational Equipment, Inc. (REI)

HARRISON ST
THOMAS ST
JOHN ST
DENNY WAY

AURORA AV N
DEXTER AV N
8TH AV N
9TH AV N
WESTLAKE AV N
TERRY AV N
BOREN AV N
FAIRVIEW AV N
MINOR AV N
PONTIUS AV N
YALE AV N
EASTLAKE AV N
BROAD ST N
5TH AV N

5TH AV
4TH AV
3RD AV
2ND AV
1ST AV
WESTERN AV
CLAY ST
CEDAR ST
VINE ST
WALL ST
BATTERY ST
BELL ST
BLANCHARD ST
LENORA ST
VIRGINIA ST
STEWART ST
HOWELL ST
OLIVE ST
PINE ST
7TH AV
6TH AV
8TH AV
9TH AV
TERRY AV
ELLIOTT AV
ALASKA WAY

Belltown P-Patch
The Old Spagetti Factory
Port of Seattle HQ
Victoria Clipper
Hotel Edgewater
Sit & Spin
Regrade Park
Crocodile Cafe
Nordstrom
Pacific Place
Monorail Station
Westlake Ctr
Westlake Ctr Food Court
Westlake Park
Bon Marche
Gameworks
City Ctr
Rainier Square
Freeway Park
Washington State Convention & Trade Ctr
HUBBELL PL
5
PIKE ST
UNION ST
UNIVERSITY ST
SENECA ST
SPRING ST
MADISON ST
MARION ST
COLUMBIA ST
CHERRY ST
JAMES ST

Anthony's at Pier 66
Odyssey Marine Discovery Center
Bell Street Pier and Bell Harbor Park
Victor Steinbrueck Park
PIKE PLACE MARKET
Park Place Market
Waterfront Trolleys
Seattle Aquarium
Seattle IMAX Dome Theatre
Bay Pavilion

Argosy Cruises
Elliott's Oyster House
Red Robin Burger & Spirits
Tillicum Village Cruise
Elliott Bay Water Taxi
Fire Station 5
Ivar's Fish Bar & Original Acres of Clams Restaurant
Let's Go Sailing
Pier 54 Adventures
Ye Olde Curiosity Shop
Coleman Dock & Riding Ferries

PIONEER SQUARE
YESLER WY
S WASHINGTON ST
S MAIN ST
S JACKSON ST
S KING ST
S LANE ST
S DEARBORN ST
5TH AV S

Pier 48
Kobe Terrace Park/ Denny Woo International District Commons
China Gate
Pho Bac
Wing Luke Asian Museum
Shanghai Garden
Uwajimaya
Bush Garden
International Children's Park

SEATTLE CENTER
▸ The Children's Museum
▸ Experience Music Project
▸ Fun Forest (rides)
▸ International Fountain
▸ Monorail Station
▸ Pacific Northwest Ballet
▸ Pacific Science Center
▸ Ride the Ducks of Seattle
▸ Seattle Center House
▸ Seattle Center Skate Park
▸ Seattle Children's Theatre
▸ Seattle Sonics and Storm
▸ Seattle Thunderbirds
▸ Space Needle

PIONEER SQUARE
▸ Bakeman's
▸ Davidson Galleries
▸ Elliott Bay Book Company
▸ Foster White Gallery
▸ Grand Central Bakery
▸ Greg Kucera Gallery
▸ Klondike Gold Rush National Park and Museum
▸ Magic Mouse Toys
▸ Metsker Maps
▸ Occidental Pedestrian Walk
▸ Seattle Mariners/Safeco Field
▸ Seattle Metropolitan Police Museum
▸ Seattle Seahawks/Seahawks Stadium
▸ Stonington Gallery
▸ Trattoria Mitchelli
▸ Underground Tour
▸ Waterfall Park
▸ Wood Shop Toys

PIKE PLACE MARKET
▸ Athenian Inn
▸ Chewing gum art wall
▸ Copacabana Restaurant
▸ Crepe de France
▸ Crumpet Shop, The
▸ Cutters Bayhouse
▸ Daily Dozen Doughnuts
▸ El Puerco Lloron
▸ F&J Great Western Trading Company
▸ Giant Shoe Museum
▸ Golden Age Collectables
▸ Grandma's Attic
▸ Great Wind Up, The
▸ Hammering Man, The
▸ Harbor Steps fountain (wading)
▸ Heritage Center and Market Tours
▸ Jack's Fish Spot and Seafood Bar
▸ Japanese Gourmet Restaurant
▸ Kells Irish Restaurant and Pub
▸ Lo Priore Brothers
▸ Market Magic Shop
▸ Market Spice
▸ Michou
▸ Parrot Market
▸ Pike Place Fish
▸ Pike Place Market
▸ Pike Place Market Creamery
▸ Pink Door, The
▸ Seattle Art Museum
▸ Seattle Garden
▸ Seattle Symphony/Benaroya Hall
▸ Sisters European Snacks
▸ Soundbridge Seattle Symphony Music Discovery Center
▸ Taxi Dogs
▸ Three Girls Sandwich Shop and Bakery
▸ Typhoon!
▸ Victor Steinbrueck Park
▸ Women's Hall of Fame

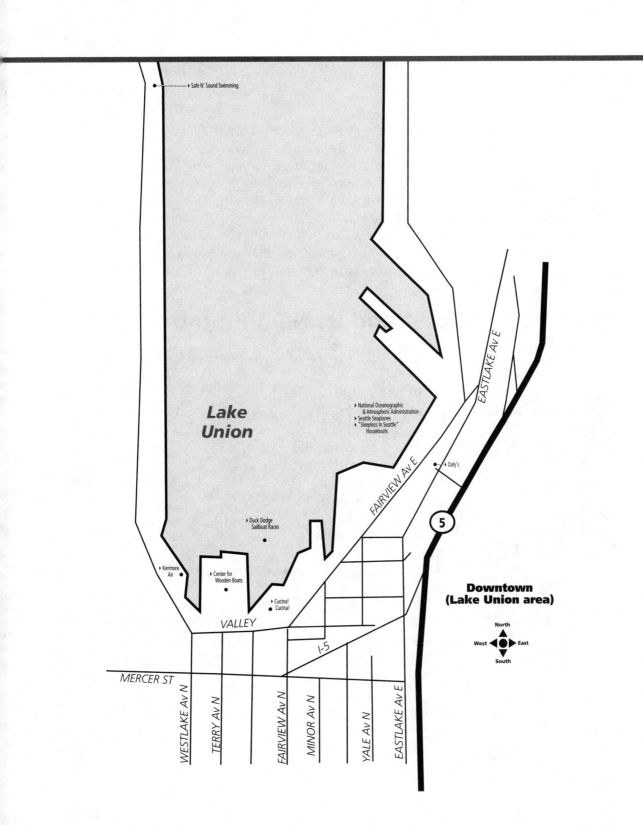

Safe N' Sound Swimming

Lake Union

National Oceanographic
& Atmospheric Administration
Seattle Seaplanes
"Sleepless in Seattle"
Houseboats

EASTLAKE AV E

FAIRVIEW AV E

Daly's

Duck Dodge
Sailboat Races

5

Kenmore
Air

Center for
Wooden Boats

**Downtown
(Lake Union area)**

Cucina!
Cucina!

VALLEY

I-5

North
West East
South

MERCER ST

WESTLAKE AV N

TERRY AV N

FAIRVIEW AV N

MINOR AV N

YALE AV N

EASTLAKE AV E

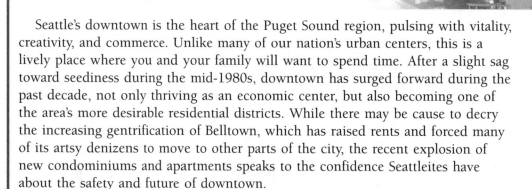

Downtown

Seattle's downtown is the heart of the Puget Sound region, pulsing with vitality, creativity, and commerce. Unlike many of our nation's urban centers, this is a lively place where you and your family will want to spend time. After a slight sag toward seediness during the mid-1980s, downtown has surged forward during the past decade, not only thriving as an economic center, but also becoming one of the area's more desirable residential districts. While there may be cause to decry the increasing gentrification of Belltown, which has raised rents and forced many of its artsy denizens to move to other parts of the city, the recent explosion of new condominiums and apartments speaks to the confidence Seattleites have about the safety and future of downtown.

Pike Place Market and Its Neighborhood

First Avenue and Pike Street
(206) 682-7453
www.pikeplacemarket.org

courtesy Nick Gunderson

Fresh produce stand at the
Pike Place Market

The Pike Place Market is the heart and soul of Seattle. Established in 1907 in response to public outrage over the price of onions, the market is today a virtual city unto itself, cramming farmers, artisans, performers, residents, retailers, restaurants, a pre-school, a medical clinic, a senior center, and a food bank into a nine-acre historic district, comprised of a maze of 15 residential and commercial buildings.

Although millions of visitors come each year to experience the sights and sounds of the market, its primary mission is to serve Seattle's downtown residents. A strict adherence to this charge is the primary reason why the market has not devolved into the hodge-

Pike Place Market

Hours: Mon.-Sat., 10 a.m. - 6 p.m.; Sun., 11 a.m. - 5 p.m. Individual business hours may vary. Closed New Year's Day, Easter Sunday, Thanksgiving Day, and Christmas.

Cost: Free

Directions: From I-5 north, take the Seneca exit (left hand exit). Take Seneca to 1st Avenue and turn right. Proceed three blocks to Pike Street. Market is on your right. *To Pike Place Market Garage* (1531 Western Avenue; free parking for up to 1 hour), take Seneca to 1st Ave. and turn left. Proceed two blocks to Madison and turn right. At Western, turn right and drive the equivalent of 5 blocks. The garage entrance is on the left.

From I-5 south, take Stewart/Denny exit and proceed on Stewart to 1st Ave. Turn left onto 1st and proceed two blocks to Pike Market is on your left. *To Pike Place Market Garage*, continue on 1st Ave. to Madison, turn right and proceed as described above.

Limited on-street meter parking ($1 per hour) or park in other pay lots.

Downtown

podge of souvenir vendors that characterize the public markets in other cities.

Always busy, the summer tourist crowds make it difficult to get around with a stroller. A back or front pack is the ideal way to navigate with little ones. Otherwise, holding hands is essential.

Under the pergola at First Avenue and Pike Street is the Market's information booth.

The least crowded times to visit are from 10:00 a.m. to noon, Monday-Thursday, January-April. If you visit during the summer – the peak tourist season – I recommend arriving as early as 9 a.m. Not only will you beat the crowds and stay cooler, but you will also experience the market as it awakens. It's fun to wander around (perhaps with a cup of coffee from the original Starbucks, where you can also get milk and juice) as the vendors set up their stalls. A breakfast treat from Three Girls Bakery or Le Panier will satisfy the appetite as you and your children explore Seattle's most prized treasure.

Unfortunately, the Market's public restrooms are not reliably clean and are sometimes downright disgusting. The restrooms available to restaurant customers are generally in much better shape.

Things to Do in the Market

Explore

This is the number one Market activity. A three-dimensional maze of day-stalls, farmer's market and shops both kooky and practical, kids of all ages love just poking around the nooks and crannies, sticking their noses into unusual stores, smelling the (mostly pleasant) odors, and generally "getting lost" in a place that mixes eras and cultures like no other.

If you want more structure, try the Heritage Trail Game. Pick up a game card at the Information Booth under the pergola at First and Pike, and then follow the "clues" that take you through the Market's lower levels.

Of course, you can always make up your own games. See how many different nations or cultures you can find represented among the stalls, vendors, and retailers. Try to identify the various languages you hear. Count the stairs between the top of the Market and the waterfront.

Those with toddlers should be warned that many of the shops in the "Down Under" section of the market contain shelves of tiny, breakable "temptations."

Downtown

Flying Fish and Live Crabs

Watch out for flying fish! Located beneath the famous neon "Public Market Center" sign and clock, you will find Pike Place Fish, a market experience you won't want to miss. When a large fish is purchased, the monger sends it flying toward the counter where his colleague deftly catches it for wrapping – a show complete with dramatic whoops, grunts, and other startling sound effects.

Across the way at Jack's Fish Spot, you will find an enormous tank of live crabs and shellfish.

I've known some tots to be squeamish around seafood, but older kids should have a blast checking out monkfish, octopus, and all kinds of ugly from the deep blue sea.

Rachel the Pig

Just in front of Pike Place Fish, under the giant neon clock, stands Rachel, the market's 550 pound bronze piggy bank, created by local artist Georgia Gerber. It's a real bank, which each year collects between $6,000 and $9,000 for the Market Foundation, a few coins at a time. Children like to ride Rachel – watch it, she's slippery. Look for Rachel's hoof prints on the sidewalk.

Enjoy the Performers

Performers at the Market range from wacky to soulful. There are 14 locations throughout the market, each marked by a musical note painted on the sidewalk, where performers display their talents. Among the regulars are á cappella groups, singer-songwriters playing acoustic instruments, Spoonman (made famous by the Soundgarden song of the same name), classical musicians, a paper-horn artist, and puppet shows. Don't forget to drop a few coins in the performer's cap if you stop to listen.

Walk the Stairs

If your child has energy to burn, you might have the right conditions for a down and back hike on the one-hundred sixty-nine steps that begin just under the clock, descend through the bowels of the market, cross Western Avenue via a skybridge, and continue all the way to the waterfront.

Downtown

Victor Steinbrueck Park

At the northwest corner of the Market sits the tiny patch of green (and spectacular Elliott Bay view) named Victor Steinbrueck Park in honor of the man who led the movement to save the Market from being replaced by a modern multi-use complex. From the railing above the Alaskan Way viaduct, you can watch the ferries make their way across the bay and enjoy the sight of Mt. Rainer (on a clear day). Two totem poles grace the park, one honoring farmers, and the other a Native American totem created by Quinault Indian artist Marvin Oliver.

While the Market strictly forbids panhandling, this is a public park and therefore outside Market Security's jurisdiction. Tourists, downtown workers, and street people generally co-exist peacefully in Victor Steinbrueck Park, but you may be hit-up for "spare change."

Post Alley

Although Post Alley runs through the entire market, there is a special subterranean appeal to the southern-most stretch of the alley, which requires that you descend the stairway that starts by Rachel the Pig under the big market clock. This cobblestone passage is home to the very disgusting and endlessly fascinating chewing gum "art wall" located outside the entrance to "Theater Sports." It started with people employing used gum to stick pennies to the wall. The pennies tend to disappear, but the gum remains, mostly in gobs, but some twisted into actual pictures. Obviously, you don't want to touch it.

Continuing down the alley, you will pass the youth hostel and find yourself face-to-face with artist Ann Sperry's galvanized steel sculpture "Seattle Garden" which portrays giant flowers sprouting along the top of the wall that surrounds a Seattle City Light facility.

Go further along the alley and you will come to the Harbor Steps development with its promenade of stairs, featuring a sort of waterfall of fountains that cascade from 1st Avenue at the top to Western at the bottom. Although it is not officially encouraged, children are often found playing in the fountains, especially the shallow stair-step one near 1st Avenue.

Downtown

Heritage Center and Market Tours

1531 Western Avenue
(206) 682-7453

The Market Heritage Center (located in the same building as the garage) is a tidy museum of Market tradition and history, featuring interactive exhibits. In addition, The Center sponsors historical lectures, cooking demonstrations, and children's activities. Call for a schedule of activities.

> **Heritage Center and Market Tours**
>
> Cost: Adults $7, children and seniors $5.
>
> Hours: Wed.-Sat., 9 a.m. (by reservation), 11 a.m & 2 p.m.; Sun., Noon & 2 p.m.

This is also the point of embarkation for Market tours. I've visited the Market hundreds of times (in fact, for several years we lived within a block), and I still discovered new things on this fascinating tour. Toddlers may be tried by this 1-hour excursion, but inquisitive older children and teenagers will enjoy themselves. Space is limited, so you will want to make a reservation.

Giant Shoe Museum

Main Arcade, Down Under

You insert coins and get to look at some pretty big shoes for a limited time. Only you can know if it's worth it to your family.

Parrot Market

1500 Western Ave.
(206) 467-6133

Although we've seen the large parrot sculpture on the sidewalk for years, we've never visited the Parrot Market. Our friend Alicia, however, recently went with her family and loved talking with – and feeding – the large selection of parrots. We'll be doing this the next time we're in the Market.

> **Parrot Market**
>
> Cost: 50¢ (refundable if you buy a parrot)

Downtown

Things to Do Near the Market

Seattle Art Museum

100 University Street
(206) 654-3255
www.seattleartmuseum.org

SAM is on par with other art museums in cities of Seattle's size – maybe better – but we all know what art museums are about. We want our kids to appreciate art, to benefit from it, to be inspired by it, but in a world of television, movies, and the Internet, it can be a painful, thankless chore to drag children in to look at paintings, sculptures, and other products of the human imagination.

Seattle Art Museum

Cost: Adults $10, student/children (7-12)/seniors $7, under 6 free. Family package (good for 2 adults and up to 4 children under 12) $30.

Hours: Tues.-Sun., 10 a.m. - 5 p.m.; Thurs., 10 a.m. - 9 p.m. Closed Mon. except during the four recurring Monday holidays – Martin Luther King Jr. Day, President's Day, Memorial Day, and Labor Day. Closed Columbus Day, Thanksgiving, Christmas Eve and Day, New Year's Eve and Day.

Directions: 2 blocks south of Pike Place Market on 1st Ave.

When Josephine was under four, SAM was one of our favorite haunts. Sometimes we would just go in to look at a single painting. We would sit on a bench in front of it and ask each other questions about what was going on: "Why do you think that woman is looking at the baby?" "He doesn't look happy, I wonder why?" "What is she drinking out of that cup?" Other times I would follow her as she cruised through the various galleries. Somewhere between 3 and 4, however, her interest waned.

We still go to SAM, but now it requires more preparation. I try to go alone first to check out new exhibits for art that will appeal to Josephine. I then start telling her about what I saw, sharing my enthusiasm for the "painting of the queen" or the "statue of the giant bunny."

Sometimes, that alone will cause her to demand a visit. If you don't have the luxury of an advance trip, take some time to study SAM's website. When the special exhibit includes works from well-known artists, I look for books containing reproductions for us to look at (both the library and SAM's museum store are good places to look). Josephine identifies with narrative, so I try (with her help) to develop a story about the paintings we are going to see.

We like to get there as early as we can and on a weekday, if possible, to avoid crowds. I don't like taking her little friends along either – too distracting.

SAM's permanent collection is naturally heavy on Northwest artists, but also includes a nice representation of European masters, as well as African, Asian, Australian, and South American artists. The museum itself is a light, inviting, modern building.

Downtown

The Hammering Man sculpture in front of the museum on First Avenue is locally popular. Call for details about special demonstrations by artists. Strollers must be checked in the lobby.

Seattle Symphony/Benaroya Hall

200 University St.
Administration: (206) 215-4700
Ticket office: (206) 215-4747
www.seattlesymphony.org

Okay, so an evening at the symphony isn't going to cut it for most children, but that doesn't mean that enjoying live classical music can't be part of your family's Seattle experience. The Seattle Symphony and Benaroya Hall offer a variety of programs designed with children in mind.

For starters, there's the extremely popular *Tiny Tots* series of dynamic, early-childhood musical performances designed for children under 6. Josephine and her grandmother greatly enjoyed dressing up for their mornings at the "symphony" (although most of the offerings are not technically "classical" or "symphonic"). Typically taking place on Tuesday or Saturday, you will want to reserve your seats well in advance. Call or check the website for the schedule.

The *Discover Music!* series on Saturday mornings is designed for older children (5-12) and is also extremely popular. These are real orchestral performances, featuring Seattle Symphony musicians and chorale singers. Pre-concert activities take place in the lobby prior to the concerts. Again, book your seats well in advance.

The *Meet the Beat* concert series is designed for the entertainment and edification of teenagers. For secondary-school band and orchestra students, the *Open Rehearsal* working sessions might be of interest. Music students will observe professional rehearsal techniques, be given an introduction to acoustics, and learn about the score being prepared and the composers. During breaks, symphony musicians, conductors, composers, or guest artists meet with students for question-and-answer sessions. The Symphony Chorale's Monday evening rehearsals are also open to music students. Call (206) 336-6650 for information.

Other musical programs are available for children seriously interested in classical music. Call or check the website for information.

If you don't have the time or inclination for performances, Benaroya Hall itself is worth the visit. Opened in 1998, Benaroya is a state-of-the-art music venue, as beautiful to the eyes as it is for the ears. Several major works of modern art were

Downtown

commissioned for the public areas of the building, including: two spectacular chandeliers by Dale Chihuly; a nine-panel, 12-foot high mural by Robert Rauschenberg; a nearly 10,000 pound steel sculpture by Mark di Suvero; and eight original drawings by Seattle artist Doris Chase. The 2,500-seat auditorium is truly stunning, not to mention acoustically excellent.

The Soundbridge Seattle Symphony Music Discovery Center (see below) is a major new addition for families interested in music.

Free tours are held on weekdays at noon and 1 p.m. Meet in the Grand Lobby entrance at the corner of Third Avenue and University Street. Group tours of 10 or more must be arranged at least 7 days in advance. Free 30-minute demonstrations of the Watjen concert pipe organ can be incorporated into your tour, but you should check the schedule first. Call (206) 215-4856 for information about tours and pipe organ demonstrations.

Soundbridge Seattle Symphony Music Discovery Center

Located in Benaroya Hall (corner of Union St. and 2nd Avenue)
(206) 336-6600
www.soundbridge.org

> **Soundbridge Seattle Symphony Music Discovery Center**
>
> Cost: Adults $7, children $5.
>
> Hours: Tues.-Sun., 10 a.m. - 6 p.m.

This is one of the coolest places for children in all of Seattle, and I'm not writing this just because its designers (Mindy Lehrman Cameron and Max Cameron) are friends of ours.

This fully interactive learning center's mission is to "inspire and nurture a love of symphonic music through active participation, exploration and creation," and it fulfills it spectacularly. Josephine loves the opportunity to try out the various orchestral instruments and is particularly enthralled by the opportunity to "conduct" the symphony herself at the "virtual conducting" station. Interactive exhibits and audio/visual presentations bring various aspects of classical music to life, including the chance to learn about musicians and composers, educational computer games, and a "Listening Bar" featuring over 500 recordings.

Soundbridge hosts student performances, demonstrations, mini-theater viewings, musical storytelling, and lectures throughout the year. Its early childhood education *Musikgarten* classes are very popular, including programs for infants and their parents through age 5, which are designed as fun, developmentally appropriate activities for children with their caretakers. Soundbridge also offers courses for parents of young children looking for ways to introduce "song, tale, and dance" into their homes. Call for details and schedules.

Downtown

Places to Shop

Grandma's Attic

Main Arcade, Down Under
(206) 682-9281
www.grandmasatticpikeplace.com

This is a fun shop for children (okay, mostly girls) who love dollies. All shapes and sizes can be found here, both new and used, including a huge selection of dollhouse accessories. There are things here for every pocketbook.

The Giving Tree Wooden Toys

Main Arcade
Phone: (206) 340-1575

Cute wooden toys. Proceeds go to the Giving Tree children's charity.

Golden Age Collectables

Main Arcade, Down Under
(206) 622-9799

This is the place for your comic book collector.

Market Magic Shop

Main Arcade, Down Under
(206) 624-4271

I'm not qualified to ascertain whether or not this shop will entertain an experienced magician, but it's perfect for children interested in mystifying their friends and family. All the classic tricks and novelty items are here.

Pike Place Market Creamery

Corner Building
(206) 622-5029

This cute little dairy market with its sneaker-wearing cows is as friendly and funky as it is tiny. There is an emphasis here on freshness and an aversion to the products of "corporate dairy farms." Check out the eggs – the last time we were there, they had ostrich, emu, and quail. Don't climb on the cows!

Downtown

Women's Hall of Fame

Main Arcade, Down Under
(206) 622-8427

This labor of love is dedicated to selling products related to important women in history and the women's movement. Slogan emblazoned t-shirts, posters, and bumberstickers are naturally available as are books, magazines, and educational games. She doesn't really understand why I do it, but I make sure to take my daughter for a quick browse whenever we're in the Market.

Market Spice

Main Arcade
(206) 622-6340

If you want to buy teas or spices, by all means shop here, but this tightly crowded space can be a challenge for little ones. You don't have to cross the threshold, however, to experience the overwhelming fragrance of the place.

F & J Great Western Trading Company

Main Arcade, Down Under
(206) 622-6376

Some things are new, some are used, some are strange, some kitschy, and some just outright creepy. Check it out.

The Great Wind Up

Economy Market Bldg.
(206) 621-9370

I'd say we buy half of our birthday presents in this toy store where almost everything must – as the name implies – be wound up. Some dance, some fly, some skitter, some crawl. There is a large table full of "tester" toys.

Downtown

"Take out" Places to Eat

The best way to eat at the Market is to put together a picnic as you explore or just graze your way through the stalls. You can get pretty much anything your mouth waters for – fresh produce, tacos and tamales, hot dogs, pasta, sandwiches, pizza, salads, stir fries, crumpets, chili, seafood, soups, sushi, and kosher – all packaged "to go." When it's not raining, Victor Steinbrueck Park makes a nice spot for a repast, as do the empty day stalls (when available) in the uncovered area north of the North Arcade. When weather doesn't permit dining al fresco, you can set up at one of the tables in the Corner Building or take up a position at one of the empty day stalls under cover in the North Arcade.

In addition to the farmer's stalls, the following are some of our favorite places from which to cobble together picnics. This list is by no means exhaustive and new, great places are springing up all the time.

The Crumpet Shop
Sanitary Market Bldg on First Ave.
(206) 682-1598

Crumpets with eggs, cheese, preserves, or Nutella; strong espresso and fine teas. On weekdays you can get fresh out-of-the-oven bread used for huge sandwiches (no sandwiches July and August).

Jack's Fish Spot and Seafood Bar
Pike Place at Post Alley
(206) 467-0514

Fresh crab, clam chowder, fresh fish, prawns, oysters, scallops and chips. Steamed clams, oysters on the half shell.

Three Girls Sandwich Shop and Bakery
Corner Market Building on Pike
(206) 622-1045

Homemade soups and sandwiches made to order, which mean you can hold the mayo, pickles, or anything else your child might object to. Also a huge offering of baked goods and pastries.

Downtown

Michou

Pike Place (Stewart House Bldg.)
(206) 448-4758

Take-out deep-dish pan pizza, panini sandwiches, assorted pasta salads, marinated vegetable salads, and many other freshly prepared Mediterranean dishes.

Crepe de France

Economy Row
(206) 624-2196

Authentic French crepes with many toothsome fillings – such as fresh strawberries and Nutella – vegetarian, and much more.

Taxi Dogs

1928 Pike Place (Soames Dunn Bldg.)
(206) 443-1919

Yummy hotdogs made from beef, pork, chicken, or turkey. Frankly (no pun intended), this is where I most often eat when I want a quick bite while shopping in the Market. Our dog Vincent likes to come with me and "share."

Lo Priore Brothers

1514 Post Alley (inside Corner Market Bldg.)
(206) 621-7545

Simple, quick Italian pasta dishes served by the most kid-engaging and all-round friendliest men in the market.

Sisters Café

1530 Post Alley (Corner Market Bldg.)
(206) 623-6723

Grilled focaccia sandwiches and hearty soups created by the three German sisters Aruna, Mariam, and Narala Jacobi.

Daily Dozen Doughnuts

Economy Row
Phone: (206) 467-7769

Mini doughnuts!!!!

Downtown

"Sit Down" Places to Eat

Although there are some fine restaurants in the market (most notably Campaigne, Chez Shea, and Il Bistro), they are expensive and not appropriate for most young children. The following are some of our favorite moderately-priced places to enjoy a sit down meal. Again, this list is far from exhaustive.

The Pink Door

1919 Post Alley
(206) 443-3241

Okay, so this isn't necessarily a moderately-priced place, but it's one of Josephine's favorite restaurants. Loved by locals and tucked into an unmarked spot denoted by the telltale color of its entrance, this funky ristoranté offers a happy marriage between world-class cuisine and family-friendly informality (the last time we were there, the hostess was wearing a giant balloon bra over her sweater). Although you wouldn't want to subject a fidgety or rowdy child to a meal here, Josephine is delighted by the "angel" motif and the small fountain in the middle of the main dining room floor. There is no children's menu, but the kitchen will gladly prepare simple pasta dishes upon request. The engaging wait staff goes out of its way to make your children feel welcome. During summer months, the dining patio with its view of Elliott Bay is a charming place for lunch. Reservations wouldn't be a bad idea, especially if you want to sit outside.

Athenian Inn

1517 Pike Place (inside the Main Arcade)
(206) 624-7166

We love this place on cold, rainy days. The food is only adequate, leaning toward the greasy spoon variety, but always hot, and the view of Elliott Bay is spectacular. Made famous by the movie *Sleepless in Seattle*, in real-life it's a modestly-priced joint where tourists rub shoulders with wizened old-timers, some of whom look as if they have been coming here since its doors first opened in 1909. Food and drink for every taste: seafood, meat, pasta, soup, salad, sandwiches, appetizers, snacks, full bar, breakfasts, espresso, ice cream, soda fountain, and (rather bizarrely, I've always thought) Filipino lunch specials.

Downtown

Japanese Gourmet Restaurant

82 Stewart Street (Stewart House Bldg.)
(206) 728-6204

The daily lunch specials here are among the best deals in town. Josephine loves eating from the "bento boxes." Yes, they also have a sushi bar. If the weather's nice, ask to be seated in the courtyard. They get you in-and-out fast.

Copacabana Restaurant

1520 1/2 Pike Place (atop the Triangle Bldg.)
Seattle, WA 98101
(206) 622-6359

Seattle's best (and possibly only) Bolivian restaurant. On a sunny day, the deck, perched above the market crowds, is the place to be. The food is quite good, although less adventurous children might have trouble finding something to eat unless previously familiar with the cuisine, which includes such temptations as spicy shrimp soup, paella, saltenas, saltados, ceviche, and mariscos.

Kells Irish Restaurant and Pub

1916 Post Alley
(206) 728-1916
www.kellsirishpub.citysearch.com

The most Irish place in town, Kells is a pub-style restaurant featuring such "comfort food" as soups, steak and kidney pie, leg of lamb, and roast chicken. The wait staff is attentive and friendly. This is another place we enjoy on stormy days. I recall one particularly cozy meal when Josephine was an infant – while she slept in a front-pack with a napkin protecting her head, I warmed myself with Irish stew as the rain beat against the windows that look out on Post Alley.

Cutters Bayhouse

2001 Western Ave. (on Victor Steinbreuck Park)
(206) 448-4884

Adjacent to the market with a sweeping view of Elliott Bay, Cutters is a large, corporate restaurant with an expansive menu designed to please every taste – from Asian to Cajun. Both kids and adults will enjoy the basket of hot focaccia bread that is served with every main course. The service is friendly and efficient. You generally will have no trouble being seated, although reservations are accepted.

Downtown

El Puerco Lloron

1501 Western Ave. (down the stairs that lead to the waterfront)
(206) 624-0541

Both the food and the ambience of this tiny, cheerful restaurant are authentic Mexican. You'll be apt to find one of the staff hand-making fresh tortillas by the door. The metal tables are emblazoned with logos for Mexican beer, and the plates, which are heaping, are usually less than $5 a pop. I love the tamales.

Typhoon!

1400 Western Avenue
(206) 262-9797
www.typhoonrestaurants.com

The third outpost of this upscale Northwest chain, Typhoon! serves a delicious menu of traditional and westernized Thai dishes. Although curries and peanut sauce may warrant some cajoling by parents, we have enjoyed many wonderful meals here with Josephine. The overall sound level is high enough to cover loud children's voices.

Pioneer Square

Pioneer Square is bordered on the south by S King St., on the west by Alaskan Way, on the north by Marion St., and by 4th Ave. S to the east.

Pioneer Square

Directions: From I-5 North or South, follow the signs to Safeco Field. You will be on Royal Brougham Way. Turn right onto 1st Ave. S. Once you've crossed King St. you are in Pioneer Square. On-street meter parking and pay lots. In the morning, there are usually metered spots available under the Alaskan Way viaduct.

This is where Seattle began. Yesler Way is the original "Skid Road," called that because loggers once let logs "skid" down the muddy avenue to the waterfront. At night, this area tends to fill up with young partiers patronizing the various taverns, nightclubs, and music venues that line its streets and alleys, but during the day it's a place where tourists rub shoulders with starving artists, entrepreneurs, and transients in one of Seattle's most colorful and sometimes edgy districts. Antique shops, restaurants, art galleries, and rug dealers occupy the ground floors of historic buildings, while the upper floors tend to serve as offices for professionals and small technology companies, as well as artist's studios and apartments.

Pioneer Square is also the place where sports fans meet before and after games. Gone is the hulking Kingdome which was replaced for baseball in 2000 by Safeco Field located just a little farther south, and for football and soccer by a new stadium (unnamed at the time of publication) scheduled to be completed in 2002.

Downtown

I met my wife in Pioneer Square and so it holds a special place in my heart. On the other hand, this is where the 2001 Mardi Gras rioting occurred, and you really can't walk a block without being solicited for "spare change." Generally speaking, however, I don't hesitate to take Josephine to Pioneer Square during the day. We tend to avoid Occidental Park because I get tired of explaining why this man is drunk or that one is sleeping on a park bench with a newspaper over his face. And, if we do find ourselves here at night, we avoid parking under the viaduct at all costs – this being the only part of Seattle that is at all known for muggings, and that only late at night.

The reasons for visiting here, however, far outweigh the reasons for staying away. The "seediness" is part of the history of this, the birthplace of Seattle, former home to loggers, trappers, gold-diggers, and mariners on shore leave – the place where the term "skid road" was first coined.

Things to Do

Klondike Gold Rush National Park and Museum

117 Main Street
(206) 553-7220
www.nps.gov/klse

**Klondike Gold Rush
National Park
and Museum**

Cost: Free

Hours: Daily, 9 a.m. - 5 p.m.

The second smallest national "park" in the country, this tiny store-front museum commemorates what is probably the most important period in the history of Seattle – the Klondike Gold Rush of 1897-98. Tens of thousands of prospectors from around the world descended upon Seattle where they loaded up on millions of dollars worth of food and supplies before steaming to Alaska to try their luck.

Along with the exhibits (such as a replica Yukon river boat and a miner's cradle), a variety of films are featured in the auditorium. Daily one-hour walking tours of the Pioneer Square historic district and gold panning demonstrations are offered by the park rangers during the summer months.

Downtown

Seattle Mariners/Safeco Field

Safeco Field is located at the corner of 1st Ave. S and Royal Brougham Way
(206) 346-4000
Mariners: 83 King Street
Seattle, WA 98104
(206) 346-4001 or 1-800-MY-MARINERS
(206) 622-HITS (tickets for both tours and games)
http://mariners.mlb.com/NASApp/mlb/sea/homepage/sea_homepage.jsp

I can imagine no better place to take in a major league baseball game than Safeco Field, which opened in 2000. Designed to evoke images of the great baseball parks of times gone by, the open air stadium with its real grass is such an incredible improvement over the now demolished Kingdome that the Seattle Mariner's past seems like the dark ages. The retractable roof is a marvel of engineering, protecting players and fans from the rain, without "enclosing" the stadium.

Seattle baseball fans are known for being polite and knowledgeable, which cannot be said of the drunken, rowdy crowds I've experienced in other cities which I shouldn't name here (Detroit, St. Louis . . .) You can walk entirely around the stadium during the game, without missing a play – in fact, fans are encouraged to do so. The bullpen area is one of our favorite stops, allowing you to stand within a few feet of the relief pitchers as they warm-up. It gives you a real sense of how hard those guys can throw.

I have mixed feelings about the children's play area. On the one hand, it's great for bored kids. On the other, once you're there, it's hard to drag them away, meaning that you can't watch the game. Ditto for the picnic and video game areas.

The tours take about one-hour and cover a distance of approximately a mile. It's fascinating to see the areas of the ballpark that are normally off-limits, such as the press box, luxury suites, field, dugouts, and visitors' clubhouse. Be forewarned, however, that some areas may be in use and therefore off-limits even to the tour. Tickets are available by calling the phone number above or on a walk-up basis at the Mariners Team Store located on the 1st Avenue side of Safeco Field.

Seattle Mariners/Safeco Field

Cost: Tours $3; games $6-$36.

Game schedule: Call or check website for schedule.

Tour hours: April 1-Oct. 31 (Baseball Season) – 10:30 a.m., 12:30 p.m. and 2:30 p.m. when the team is on the road (the 2:30 p.m. tour is canceled when the team plays at home). Nov. 1-Mar 31 (Baseball's Offseason) – Tues.-Sun., 12:30 p.m. and 2:30 p.m. Holiday hours may vary so call for details.

Downtown

Pioneer Place

Yesler Way & 1st Ave. S

Pioneer Place

Cost: Free

The motto for this tiny park in the heart of Pioneer Square marking Seattle's first permanent settlement should be "everything is replaceable."

The original totem pole at this location was stolen from the Tlingit Native American tribe in 1890 by a bunch of drunken pioneers, burned by an arsonist in 1938, then replaced with the current pole carved by the same tribe from which it was originally taken. The ornate Pergola, originally built in 1905 to protect cable-car passengers from the rain, was demolished by a tractor-trailer in 2001, and was recently replaced by the current structure. The Victorian-Romanesque Pioneer Building, which is on the east side of the park, was built in 1892, itself a replacement for the original building that was destroyed in the Great Fire of 1889. As far as I know, the Chief Seattle drinking fountain is an original . . .

Underground Tour

600 1st Ave.
(206) 682-4646
www.undergroundtour.com

Underground Tour

Cost: Adults $9, seniors $7, children (7-12) $5, under 7 free.

Hours: May-Sept., schedule varies by month. Call for current times. Reservations highly recommended.

Starting at Doc Maynard's Public House, this 90-minute tour of underground Seattle is one of the city's most popular and unusual attractions. The guided tour takes you through subterranean old Seattle, below today's street-level, through the remains of the original town on top of which Seattle was rebuilt (due to poor drainage) after the Great Fire of 1889. It's fascinating, hokey, and a little spooky all at the same time.

Kids under 6 will likely start to complain before you're finished with the 20-minute presentation that precedes the tour. They are also apt to gripe about the cold, damp and dark, as well as the rough terrain and steep climbs of the tour itself.

On the other hand, older kids will likely consider this to be their favorite Seattle activity.

Bringing your own flashlight is a good idea.

Downtown

Occidental Pedestrian Walk

Occidental Ave. S between S Washington St. and S Jackson St.

Frankly, the north half of this two block long "pedestrian walk" (most commonly referred to as "Occidental Park") tends to be a congregating place for street alcoholics. In spite of efforts by merchants and the police, I've often felt nervous here, especially in the afternoon and evening.

There are two totem poles: the tall one called *Sun and Raven* and a smaller Kwakiutl totem bear carved by artist Duane Pasco. The Seattle Fallen Firefighters memorial stands at the intersection of Occidental and S Main, featuring life-size bronze sculptures of firefighters at work. This is also where you will find a trolley station from which you can get to the International District or the waterfront.

The southern half of the park (between S Main and S Jackson) is far less threatening and is home to many art galleries (see below).

> **Occidental Pedestrian Walk**
> Cost: Free

Waterfall Park

S Main St. and 2nd Ave. S

This tiny, privately maintained and managed park with its refreshing waterfall fountain is a pleasant place for a picnic or just to escape for a moment from the city. You'll need to watch your smaller children closely – it would be easy to fall in.

> **Waterfall Park**
> Cost: Free

Seattle Seahawks/Seahawks Stadium

Occidental Ave. S, between S King and S Royal Brougham
(1-800) NFL-HAWK (tickets)
www.seahawks.com

By the time this book is published, the new Seahawk Stadium will be home to Seattle's NFL franchise and – in all likelihood – have a new name. Information about stadium tours was unavailable at the time of publication.

> **Seattle Seahawks/ Seahawks Stadium**
> Cost: $15-$68, children under 3 are free.
> Schedule: Call for scheduled home games or visit the web site.

Seattle Metropolitan Police Museum

317 Third Ave. S
(206) 748-9991
www.members.aol.com/smpmuseum

The largest police museum in the western U.S., it is designed to educate children of all ages. The children's area features coloring books, a jail cell, a police "communications center," and an opportunity to dress-up in real police uniforms. Be forewarned that these uniforms include gun belts and bulletproof vests, which may be objectionable to some parents.

> **Seattle Metropolitan Police Museum**
> Cost: Adults $3, children (under 12) $1.50.
> Hours: Tues.-Sat., 11 a.m. - 4 p.m.

Downtown

Places to Shop

Magic Mouse Toys

603 1st Avenue S
(206) 682-8097

If you don't let your child drag you in here, you must have a heart of stone. My first Magic Mouse experience was at the side of my nephew Ian (then 12) who took me on a tour of the gamers section. Josephine is more interested in the large selection of dolls, stuffed animals, and art/craft supplies. The train area (both electric and wooden) has always struck me as particularly well-stocked.

There is an emphasis here on toys and games you won't find at Toys R Us.

Elliott Bay Book Company

101 S Main Street
(206) 624-6600
www.elliottbaybook.com

Seattle is a notoriously "bookish" city (probably because the fall and winter weather are so conducive to curling up with a good read), and Elliott Bay Book Company is the heart and soul of its literary life. Even Jeff Bezos – the CEO of online bookseller Amazon.com – has been known to rhapsodize about this rambling, maze-like brick-and-mortar bookstore.

The staff is knowledgeable and the children's section well-stocked with both contemporary books and classics. The used book section is a great place to check for bargains and out-of-print titles (including children's books).

Toddlers (and even some adults) can easily get lost in here, so hold hands!

Readings by authors and signings are free, but very popular – tickets are sometimes required. Children's readings are typically on weekends. Call for schedules.

The basement café offers soups, sandwiches, and a place to get started on your new purchases.

Wood Shop Toys

320 First Ave. S
(206) 624-1763

"Jack," a wooden statue that looks a little like a giant marionette, beckons you into this store where only wooden toys from all over the world live. You won't find any corporate toys here – just the real things.

Downtown

Art Galleries

Throughout Pioneer Square

Although some have relocated in recent years, Pioneer Square still has the highest concentration of art galleries in the region. It's the rare child who can handle an afternoon of looking at art, but Josephine and I enjoy dropping into a gallery or two whenever we're in the area. We have fun making up stories about the paintings (most often it's Josephine who has the more profound insights), or choosing our favorites.

Naturally, only you know your own child. If she can't be trusted to not touch, run, climb, or shriek, then you might want to skip the galleries. Typically, we invite our daughter to look through the windows, and only if she wants to see more, do we go in.

New shows are previewed on what's called "first Thursday" (first Thursday of each month, except during the summer). Pioneer Square, and particularly the south end of the Occidental Pedestrian Walk (see above), takes on a sort of festival atmosphere as crowds come down to checkout the new shows. We don't recommend this for families with young children.

Davidson Galleries

313 Occidental Ave.
(206) 624-7684
www.davidsongalleries.com

Features contemporary Northwest painters as well as a select group I of international artists.

Foster White Gallery

123 S Jackson St.
(206) 622-2833
www.fosterwhite.com

Our daughter says the Dale Chihuly glass art makes her feel like she's in a fairyland. When I win the lottery, I'm going to buy her one.

Stonington Gallery

119 S Jackson St.
(206) 405-4040
www.stoningtongallery.com

Native American art and jewelry.

Downtown

Greg Kucera Gallery

212 3rd Ave. S
(206) 624-0770
www.gregkucera.com

Exhibits contemporary paintings, sculpture, and works on paper by nationally recognized artists and artists of the Northwest.

Metsker Maps

702 1st Ave. S
(1-800) 727-4430 or (206) 623-8747
www.metskermaps.com

> **Metsker Maps**
>
> Hours: Mon.-Fri. 9 a.m. - 6 p.m.,
> Sat. 10 a.m. - 5 p.m.

Even if my "cousin" Larry didn't work here, I'd include Metsker Maps in this guide. If you're not in the market for maps, atlases, globes, charts, travel books, outer space "stuff," or CD-ROMs, it's still worth poking your head in here. You and your family will discover many things you didn't even know you wanted, and the staff is as friendly as they come.

Places to Eat

There are lots of places to eat and snack in Pioneer Square, although not many in the gourmet category (with the notable exception of Il Terrazzo Carmine, which is not a great place for children). These are the places we patronize when in Pioneer Square.

Bakeman's

122 Cherry St.
(206) 622-3375

This is the first place to which I was taken for lunch when I arrived in Seattle in 1984. The line curled through the cafeteria-style dining room, out the door, and up the stairs to the sidewalk. My companion kept saying, "Make sure you know what you want when it's your turn to order." It was rather intimidating. The line – as I've learned it always does – moved fast, and sure enough, I was flustered to find it was suddenly my turn to order.

Here's the tip: turkey on white or wheat, with mayo and cranberry. The meatloaf and turkey noodle soup are the other sure things. Finish it off with carrot cake.

Downtown

Trattoria Mitchelli

84 Yesler Way
(206) 623-3883

I was first introduced to authentic espresso drinks at this popular Italian joint when I was single. Then, I thought of it as a cool place for a late night drink or a groggy morning-after breakfast.

Now, we all enjoy the breakfast, lunch, and dinner menus, which feature a huge number of family-friendly pastas, pizzas, and other Italian staples. The service is prompt, prices reasonable, and – most importantly – Josephine loves the food.

Grand Central Bakery

214 1st Ave. S
(206) 622-3644

It's the cinnamon rolls that draw us into this artisan bakery, especially when they are warm out of the oven. For lunch, the soups are good, but it's the sandwiches on incredible bread that steal the show. On cold, rainy days, try to get a seat by the fire.

International District

The district is bounded by Yesler Way on the north,
Dearborn Avenue on the south,
IInterstate-5 on the east, and 5th Avenue S on the west.

This compact district, just east of Pioneer Square and south of downtown, is often called Chinatown, although it is better known to locals as the International District, a more appropriate name given that it is one of the few places in America where immigrants from not only China, but from all over Asia, the Pacific Islands, and Africa have settled together to build a single, unified neighborhood. If the truth be told, the International District long ago overflowed its "formal" boundaries, spreading under the freeway eastward, turning right on Rainier, and expanding more or less throughout Seattle's south end. You can find Asian restaurants, groceries, and sundry shops along the length of Rainier Ave. and Martin Luther King Jr. Way and across the crest of Beacon Hill.

International District

Directions: From I-5 north, take the Safeco Field/4th Ave. exit. Turn right on 4th, then right on Jackson St. to 5th Ave., which puts you at the western edge of the district. From I-5 south, take the Dearborn exit. Turn right on Dearborn, then right on 7th Ave., which puts you at the northern edge of the district. Limited on-street parking and pay lots.

Downtown

courtesy Wing Luke Museum

Dragon at Wing Luke Museum

The cultural heart of the city's Asian-American community, the International District is home to an array of exotic groceries, shops, restaurants, and other businesses offering all manner of Asian specialties. The International District, above all, is a residential district where locals live in apartments above storefronts and congregate in the area's urban parks such as Hing Hay, Kobe Terrace, or the International Children's Park. This isn't one of those neon-emblazoned, tourist traps, but a *genuine* neighborhood. As a result, there are, in fact, few "tourist attractions" here, but much to enjoy as you peruse this urban melting pot.

One of our favorite itineraries for the I.D. is to start off by exploring Kobe Terrace Park (see below). When we're finished here, we follow 7th Ave. S to the Wing Luke Museum (see below), have lunch next door at Pho Bac (see below), then continue down the street to the International Children's Park (see below) for an hour or so of play. It's a cheap, entertaining, and educational way to spend morning and afternoon.

Mariners and Seahawks games tend to create traffic jams and to soak up all available parking, so check the team schedules before trekking into the International District.

courtesy Army Corps of Engineers

Enjoying the sun at an event in one of Seattle's many parks

Downtown

Things to Do

Kobe Terrace Park/
Denny Woo International District Community Garden

221 6th Ave. S (follow 7th Avenue north until it ends at S Main St.)
www.cityofseattle.net/parks

From 7th Avenue, we like to climb through the steep stairs, winding boardwalks, and bridges that take us through the elaborate hillside community gardens. When it's not pouring rain, you will find residents working the soil or just sitting on a bench in a peaceful island of shade or sun. The top is marked by a giant stone lantern that in summer months sits in the midst of a shallow pool of water. Don't be surprised to find individuals or groups quietly involved in martial arts exercises in this lovely spot.

Chinatown Discovery Tours

P.O. Box 3406
Seattle, WA 98114
(425) 885-3085

courtesy Chinatown Discovery Tours
Walking Tour

Reservations are necessary for any of the tour packages with prices ranging up to $40 per person (dim sum lunch included) and lasting as long as 3 hours. Most appropriate for families with youngsters, however, is the fabulous "Touch of Chinatown" walking tour, which is the least expensive and at 1 hour, won't tax your child's patience. Most children over, say 5, will be fascinated to learn how fortune cookies and other Asian specialties are made. An Asian Youth Program tour, which is designed for students in grades 1-12, is also available for groups.

Chinatown Discovery Tours

Cost: Adults $12.95, children $7.95.

Hours: Call for tour reservations

Downtown

International Children's Park

Seventh Ave. S and S Lane St.

A charming playground. Younger children will enjoy playing here with the neighborhood youngsters. Built in 1981, the park incorporates both traditional and contemporary Asian design, including a neon-bedecked pavilion and a stair-step shaped dragon (slippery when wet, and hot when sunny) designed by Seattle sculptor Gerard Tsutakawa. The swinging bridge is a hit as are the climbing rocks. Don't be deceived by the small size of this park – it's fun.

Wing Luke Asian Museum

407 Seventh Avenue S
(206) 623-5124
www.wingluke.org

courtesy Wing Luke Museum

Korean drummer

Named for Wing Luke, the first Asian Pacific American elected official in the Pacific Northwest, this museum is the only Pan-Asian museum in the U.S. dedicated to the collection, preservation, and display of Asian American culture, history, and art. The centerpiece of the museum is its "One Song, Many Voices" exhibit which includes photos and artifacts from early Asian culture in the Northwest. Even the youngest children are delighted by the interactive nature of the exhibit, allowing little fingers to handle many of the more interesting items and to try on festival costumes worn by early Asian settlers.

Older children, especially those with a social conscience, may want to explore the "The Densho: Japanese American Legacy Project," an interactive, multimedia archive that captures, shares, and preserves the experiences of Japanese Americans before, during, and after WWII, with a special emphasis on the thousands who were unjustly incarcerated during the war. Two computer workstations are available.

The museum also hosts temporary exhibits that are typically very well done.

Wing Luke Asian Museum

Cost: Adults $4, students/seniors $3, children (5-12) $2. Tour fee $2.50 per person. First Thursdays of every month are free.

Hours: Tues.-Fri., 11 a.m. - 4:30 p.m.; Sat.-Sun., 12 p.m. - 4 p.m.

Downtown

Places to Shop

You'll likely want to wander around sticking your head into the various mom-and-pop operations throughout the I.D., but as far as destination shopping goes, there is one place above all others, and that is . . .

Uwajimaya

600 5th Ave. S
(206) 624-6248
www.uwajimaya.com

Uwajimaya

Hours: Mon.-Sat., 8 a.m. - 11p.m.; Sun., 9 a.m. - 10 p.m.

Uwajimaya is just your average supermarket – that is if you hail from a large Asian city. The Pacific Northwest's leading Asian grocery and gift retailer, we especially love our visits to the new International District location of this exciting, exotic store with its piles of unrecognizable vegetables and aisles of fascinating imported packaged goods. Check out the fish department for a real eye-opening (and sometimes stomach churning) experience (my daughter still can't pass the fish counter with her eyes open). Do you dare find out what's lurking in the tub of brine? The gift store features a lively selection of items, including wonderful toys and dolls, and separate book, cosmetics, and electronic departments that feature top Asian brands, as well as numerous hot food kiosks that tempt shoppers with take-out delicacies from across the Pacific.

Children of every age will want to take a walk down the cookie and cracker aisle – these are treats unlike any they've ever seen in traditional American supermarkets.

Downtown

Places to Eat

I doubt that anyone knows exactly how many restaurants there are in the I.D., and I'm sure that there are many as good as those listed below, but these are wonderful options.

China Gate Restaurant

516 7th Avenue S
(206) 624-1730

> **China Gate Restaurant**
> Hours: Daily, 10 a.m. - 2 a.m.

From a decorator's point-of-view, this is a big Americanized version of a Chinese restaurant, designed to appeal to tourists and Asian food neophytes. That said, I've yet to have better dim sum anywhere, and the Szechwan and Cantonese menu is as good as it is expensive.

For those unfamiliar, dim sum are small (think bite-sized) portions of various Chinese dishes that ultimately add-up to a full meal. Waitresses pass among tables with carts bedecked with steamed, baked, and stir-fried delicacies, and you pick-out what appeals to you. Josephine loves eating this way – it gives her a real sense of control, and she often winds up eating things she never would have chosen from a menu. Of course, there is also the "creep-out" factor that comes from spotting something with thick, slimy tentacles or staring eyes, which can be either a horror or delight depending on your child's disposition. Traditionally, dim sum is only served as a sort of weekend brunch, but China Gate offers it for lunch daily and as a late-night dinner.

The live fish tanks are not just for decoration – these contain the main ingredients of China Gate's seafood dishes. You may pick your own crab, shrimp, or sea bass from the tank or let the wait staff do it for you. Either way, you know it's fresh.

The menu is huge, so if after considering the fish tanks you've decided to become a vegetarian for the day, there are plenty of alternatives.

Downtown

Pho Bac

415 Seventh Ave. S
(206) 621-0532
and
1314 S Jackson St. (east of I-5 at Boren)
(206) 323-4387

Pho Bac

Hours: Seventh Ave. location –
Mon., Wed.-Sun., 11 a.m. -
Midnight; closed Tues.

S Jackson location – daily,
10 a.m. - 9 p.m.

These two Vietnamese soup joints might be my favorite lunch spots in Seattle. Words are inadequate to describe the rich, complexly flavored beef broth that bathes noodles and thinly sliced beef, tripe, or meatballs that arrives on your table within minutes. Josephine and I like to hold our faces over our bowls for a fragrant, culinary steam bath, before adding our own fresh basil, cilantro, bean sprouts, and chilies, then digging in. Chicken soup is also available and also fantastic. Best of all, the price is right – a large bowl ($5.50) easily makes a meal for two children (ask for extra bowls as necessary). Unless you're very hungry, stick with a medium bowl ($4.50).

The Seventh Avenue location is next door to the Wing Luke Asian Museum (see above) with only a dozen or so tables, all of which are full by noon. If you show up by 11:45, however, you probably won't have a wait. The S Jackson Street location (follow Jackson St. east, under the freeway to where it intersects with Boren – it's the triangular building on the right) is the original Pho Bac.

Shanghai Garden

524 6th Ave. S
(206) 625-1689

Shanghai Garden

Hours: Sun.-Thurs.,
11 a.m. - 9:30 p.m.;
Fri.-Sat., 11 a.m. - 10:30 p.m.

Generally considered to be Seattle's best traditional Chinese restaurant, it is the opposite of China Gate (see above) in that it caters largely to a Chinese clientele. The shaven-noodles are very popular. Lunchtime can be extremely busy.

Bush Garden

614 Maynard Ave. S
(206) 682-6830

Bush Garden

Hours: Mon.-Sat.,
5 p.m. - 10 p.m.;
Sun. 5 p.m. - 9 p.m.

You might get better Japanese food elsewhere, but your children will love the colorful, elaborate décor. A stream with a footbridge runs through the place.

Downtown

Retail Core

**Bordered by Virginia Street to the north,
Seneca to the South,
2nd Ave. to the west,
and 7th Ave. to the east.**

Retail Core

Directions: From I-5 north, take the Union St. exit (#165B) and start looking for a pay lot or one of the rare on-street metered parking spots. From I-5 south, take the Seneca St. exit (#165) and do as above. We usually park in the Pacific Place parking garage. From either of these exits, turn right on 6th Ave. Proceed on 6th for a few blocks (2 or 4 depending on which exit you took) until you cross Pine St. The entrance to the garage is on the right near the end of the block.

If you're a shopper, you will have found this area without my help. Home to the Nordstrom flagship store, The Bon Marche, Niketown, Pacific Place, Westlake Center, and hundreds of other national and local retailers, this is where we go to empty out our wallets. It's a place to wander around, poking your nose into shops and shopping centers, taking in a movie or grabbing a bite.

You will certainly find most of the national retailers that appeal to families here, but our focus is on some of the more unique offerings in Seattle's retail core.

Things to Do

Gameworks

**1511 7th Ave. (7th and Pike St.)
(206) 521-0952
www.gameworks.com**

Gameworks

Cost: Free

Hours: Mon.-Thurs., 11 a.m. - 12 a.m.; Fri., 11 a.m. - 1 a.m.; Sat., 10 a.m. - 1 a.m.; Sun., 10 a.m. - 12 a.m. (No one under 18 admitted after 10 p.m.)

Yes, you can find Gameworks in other cities, but it's such a mecca for youths, it would be a true omission to leave it out.

When Gameworks first opened in 1997, we were living only a few blocks away, and I dropped in every chance I got, usually at 11 a.m. before the crowds arrived – and man, it can get crowded later in the day. This two-story temple to state-of-the-art video and virtual reality gaming is simply too loud and dark for young children, but adolescents and teenagers will want to live here.

While the racecar game is a blast, and I've been known to work up a sweat on the snowboard, I personally prefer the "vintage" games upstairs, which is where you'll find us old guys.

Downtown

Freeway Park/Washington State Convention and Trade Center
Between Seneca St. and Pike St. over I-5

Built in 1976, Freeway Park was considered at the time to be the epitome of brilliant urban land use, built as it was over Interstate 5. It's showing its age a bit, but remains a cool place to explore with kids during the day (I'm wary of the place at night). The highlight is the manmade landscape of waterfall and canyon. Children love to hike the "trail" from top to bottom, but you'll want to go with them – both because it's fun and because it's not unusual to run into seedy characters along the way.

The Washington State Convention and Trade Center joined Freeway Park over the 12 lanes of I-5 in the mid-1980s. The building itself is fascinating, but the surrounding grounds are the kind of architecture that even young children can appreciate. Blending urbanity with nature, it is an adventure to wander the walkways and stairways, while admiring the public art. Our favorite is "Seattle George" by artist Buster Simpson – no matter where you stand, you still see George Washington in profile.

The indoor art gallery is open daily from 5 a.m. to Midnight.

Westlake Park
Pine St. and 4th Ave.

During the holidays, a giant carousel is operated here, but otherwise the main attraction for children is the waterfall fountain. Josephine can't resist walking "under" the loud waterfall on the walkway provided for just that purpose. Actually, she'll only go through holding my hand, which means we both get wet every time. The fountain is turned off during the winter.

Mt. Rainier rises in the distance.

Downtown

Monorail

Westlake Center to Seattle Center campus
Pine St. and 5th Ave.
(206) 441-6038
www.seattlemonorail.com

Monorail

Fares (one-way): Adults $1.25, children (5-12) and seniors 50¢, under 5 free.

Hours: Mon.-Fri., 7:30 a.m. - 11 p.m.; Sat.-Sun., 9 a.m. - 11 p.m.

Across the street from Westlake Park is the Westlake Center indoor shopping mall. Take the escalators to the top floor for the Monorail station.

As far as Josephine is concerned, we could just ride the monorail back-and-forth all day. Another vestige of the 1962 World's Fair, the monorail leaves every 10 minutes, taking you to Seattle Center in 2 minutes.

Try to get the seat by the driver.

Places to Eat

There are many restaurants in the area, although since they mainly cater to the downtown office crowd, none of them really stand out as family-oriented establishments. The only real recommendation we have is the food court on the top floor of Westlake Center (Pine and 4th) – here you are certain to find options for every taste.

Places to Shop

The following is an incomplete listing of some of the main shopping venues that are of interest to families:

Nordstom, department store, Pine and 4th

The Bon Marche, department store, Pine and 3rd

Niketown, active sports wear, Pike and 6th

Westlake Center, indoor mall (Monorail station upstairs), Pine and 4th

Pacific Place, indoor mall, Pine and 6th

Banana Republic, clothing, Pike and 5th

City Center, indoor mall (including FAO Schwartz), Pike and 6th

Rainier Square, indoor mall, Union and 4th

Old Navy, clothing, Pine and 6th

Eddie Bauer, outdoor clothing and equipment, Union and 5th

Downtown

Cascade Neighborhood

This tiny neighborhood is tucked between I-5 and Fairview Ave. to the east and west, and N Mercer St. and N Denny Way to the north and south.

The Convention and Visitor's Bureau will not direct you here, nor will most tourist guides or people you stop on the street. To most Seattleites, this is a dead little corner of downtown (aside from REI), given over to warehouses, cheap apartments, and a little light industry. But after you've had your fill of REI, weather permitting, take a walk around – there's more to see than first meets the eye.

You get here by following the directions to REI (below). All of the attractions listed here are within a few blocks of each other. Free on-street parking.

Recreational Equipment, Inc. (REI)

222 Yale Ave. N
(206) 223-1944 or (888) 873-1938 (toll free)
www.rei.com

courtesy REI

The REI flagship store is the best indoor playground – for children and adults – in the city. We've often met friends here for play-dates with no intention of buying anything (although we usually do).

The first thing you'll notice is the 3-story rock-climbing boulder. Generally, this is for older children (over about 7), but our friend Emily has been climbing it since she was 4-years-old. The cost for a single climb is $3 (members) or $8 (non-members). Ten-climb punch cards are also available.

Upstairs in the children's department is a slide made to look like a canoe and another that looks like a hollow tree, a cave complete with hibernating bears, and a plastic pond. In the

Downtown

Recreational Equipment, Inc. (REI)

Hours: Mon.-Fri., 10 a.m. - 9 p.m.; Sat., 10 a.m. - 7 p.m.; Sun., 11 a.m. - 6 p.m.

Directions: From I-5 north, take Olive Way exit (#166). Follow Olive Way east to Bellevue Ave. Turn left on Bellevue and left on Denny Way. Cross over the freeway, then turn right on Pontius Ave. and right again on Thomas St. REI is on the right. From I-5 south, take the Stewart St. exit (#166). Stewart crosses Yale Ave. N. Take a right on Yale. REI is one block north. Free parking in REI's garage. Entrance on Yale.

footwear department, you'll find a short, rocky hiking trail for testing boots. If you're bicycle shopping, the outdoor riding trail is both a good test for the equipment and the rider.

REI also offers a wide range of clinics and events for all ages. Call or check the website for a schedule and prices.

courtesy REI

Rock Climber

Oh yeah, REI also sells everything for outdoor recreation, be it hiking, camping, cycling, boating, winter sports, climbing, or just keeping warm. The products are as good as you'll get anywhere. If you intend to buy a lot or want to take advantage of the clinics and/or special events, membership is a good investment.

My only complaint is that it's sometimes frustrating to get help from salespeople.

Cascade P-Patch

Minor Ave. N and Thomas Street

This cute community garden is special in that a sizeable percentage of the water used comes from its inventive rainwater collection system. The system collects rain from specially designed "collector traps" and from the roofs of nearby buildings, channeling it into 55-gallon barrels. Take a close look: can you find the traps? An informative sign is here detailing how it works. Adjacent to the P-Patch you will find the Cascade People's Center, a funky, little facility that offers classes and childcare for families.

Downtown

Cascade Playground

333 Pontius Ave. N
www.ci.seattle.wa.us/parks/parkspaces/cascade.htm

It's nothing special when you consider it in the context of all the parks in the city, but finding 1.9 acres here in the urban jungle is like a breath of fresh air for families seeking a safe, outdoor playground for their restless brood. The playground equipment is relatively new and separated from the street by a fence. The adjacent Cascade P-Patch (see above) is an added attraction.

There are at least two private schools of which I'm aware that use this park during the day, and as such, the bathrooms tend to be kept in pretty good shape.

St. Spiridon Orthodox Cathedral

400 Yale Ave. N (corner of Yale and Harrison)
www.saintspiridon.org
(206) 624-5341

courtesy St. Spiridon Orthodox Cathedral

St. Spiridon Orthodox Cathedral

This cathedral with its blue "onion" domes and gold crosses is like something from the Byzantine Empire, although it wasn't built until 1937 (the Russian Orthodox/Greek Catholic congregation has been in Seattle since 1895). Check out the beautiful brass bells by the entrance on the Harrison side.

The inside of the church is rich in traditional physical symbols such as icons, crosses, burning candles, and incense. Although formal tours are not offered, you are invited to join the congregation at its beautiful services. Call or consult the website for times.

Taco Del Mar Corporate Headquarters Artwork

434 Yale Ave N (corner of Yale and Republican)
(206) 624-7060

While in the neighborhood, have a look at the funky urban sculpture along the Republican side of the headquarters of this tasty local chain of fish taco restaurants. Running the length of the building, the sculpture incorporates benches, a system of troughs through which (it appears) rainwater can flow, galvanized steel tubs, tubes, rocks, plants, and concrete.

Downtown

Seattle Center

Bordered by 5th Ave. N, Denny Way, 1st Ave. N, and Mercer St.
Customer Services (206) 684-7200/TDD/TYY: (206) 684-7100
24-Hour Automated Events Line: (206) 684-8582
Transportation Hotline: (206) 233-3989
www.seattlecenter.com

Seattle Center

Cost: Free, although many of the attractions have separate admission.

Hours: 24 hours a day, 7 days a week.

Directions: From I-5 north or south, take the Mercer Street exit (from I-5 north it is a left hand exit). Follow the signs to Seattle Center. Street and lot parking are available. From downtown (Westlake Center at 5th and Pine), the monorail is a 2-minute ride.

Home to the Space Needle, Pacific Science Center, Children's Museum, Seattle Supersonics and Storm basketball teams, Seattle Children's Theater, Experience Music Project, and dozens of other attractions, a family could easily spend an entire week at Seattle Center and still not run out of new things to do.

My family is here at least once a week, attending ballet classes, taking in a play, enjoying a musical performance, or just horsing around in the Children's Museum. It's a place I rarely visited BC (Before Child), but now I don't know how we could live without it.

The site of the 1962 World's Fair, the 74-acre campus was constructed using the theme "Century 21: The World of Tomorrow," which explains the Jetson-like sensibility of our city's most recognizable symbol – the Space Needle. While some of the original "space-age" architecture was temporary by nature, enough of it remains (such as the International Fountain or the science center's arches and reflection pools) that you get the feeling that you're in a bizarre kind of time warp where the past and its perceptions of the future co-exists with the reality of the present.

Trying to do everything in one visit is impossible, so if time is limited, pick out two or three things and do them well. Make sure to call the events hotline (listed above) before planning your visit. The center hosts dozens of special events over the course of the year (especially during the summer), which you will either want to attend or avoid. Be aware, also, that some attractions – such as the Fun Forest amusement park rides – are only open seasonally, so call first.

Restrooms are plentiful, safe and – mostly – clean. During weekends and holidays, attractions can get crowded. We enjoy Seattle Center the most on weekday mornings and early afternoons.

Downtown

Things to Do

Space Needle

Seattle Center campus
(206) 905-2100

The Space Needle!

The Space Needle is the classic example of a place that locals only visit with out-of-town guests. I spent a lot of time on the Skyline Level (the Space Needle's banquet and catering facility) during my years at the chamber of commerce, but have only been to the observation level a handful of times during the past few years.

As a visitor, however, you and your family will want to take the 43-second, 520 foot glass elevator ride up the stem of the structure to enjoy the fantastic 360-degree view from the enclosed observation area.

Just below the observation level is the SkyCity revolving restaurant, featuring Northwest cuisine. The restaurant makes a complete revolution every 48 minutes, which is a great way to take in the entire view at your leisure, but will feel painfully slow to your children who will – whatever you tell them in advance – be expecting to eat on some sort of merry-go-round. If dining at the restaurant, your elevator ride is free. Be forewarned that SkyCity is not an inexpensive restaurant.

Space Needle gifts and souvenirs are available on the Pavilion Level on the ground floor.

Space Needle

Cost: Adult $11, senior $9, youth (age 11-17) $8, child (5-12) $5, 4 and under free. (To be seated in the dining area, each guest age 11 and over must purchase $15 for lunch and $25 for dinner excluding alcohol to avoid the elevator charge.)

Hours: Observation deck open Mon.-Sun., 8 a.m. - Midnight; restaurant open Mon.-Sun., 10 a.m. - 2:45 p.m. and 4:30 p.m. - 10:15 p.m. Brunch Sat.-Sun., 8 a.m. - 2:45 p.m. Open 365 days a year.

Downtown

Fun Forest

Just to the west and north of the Space Needle on Seattle Center grounds.
(206) 728-1586
www.funforest.com

Fun Forest

Cost: Ride costs vary; 6 hour pass $18.

Season/Hours: June - Labor Day – Daily, 11 a.m. - Midnight; Spring & Fall – Fri., 7 p.m. - 11 p.m.; Sat., Noon - 11 p.m.; Sun., Noon - 8 p.m.; Winter – outside rides closed. Entertainment Pavilion open daily year round at 11 a.m.

Try as I might, I can't entirely avoid the Fun Forest with its 19 permanent rides, games, and attendant surly "carnie" employees. The rides for younger children are separated from the "scream machines" that older kids favor, including a Ferris wheel, a classic merry-go-round, and junior versions of the bumper cars, the roller coaster, and other rides. Older children will gravitate toward the rides with names like Windstorm (roller coaster), Wild River (log ride), and Orbiter.

The Entertainment Pavilion is an indoor facility that houses a fun mini-golf course, laser tag, video games, and some rides.

Everyone will have fun, but I'm always taken aback by how expensive it gets buying tickets one-ride-at-a-time. The kiddy rides are $2-$3 a pop. If you're going to be here any length of time, if you are riding with your children, or if you have older children (who will want to partake in the more expensive rides), the $18, 6-hour pass is the way to go.

The Children's Museum

Lower Level of the Center House
(206) 441-1768
www.thechildrensmuseum.org

The Children's Museum

Cost: $5.50 per person.

Hours: Mon.-Fri., 10 a.m. - 5 p.m.; Sat.-Sun., 10 a.m. - 6 p.m.

We would wear out our Children's Museum membership card with how often we visit if it wasn't for the fact that the front desk crew knows us so well they just wave us through.

With eight permanent galleries, one temporary gallery, and three studio spaces, this is a fantastic way to spend a few hours or an entire morning – especially on a rainy day – with children up to about 8-years-old.

The Mountain Forest exhibit is designed to educate children about Washington state's natural habitat as they play dress-up in hiking gear or animal costumes, camp-out in a tent, slide down the "glacier" slide, or sneak through a cave full of bats and flowing lava.

Downtown

We've spent hours in the Cog City exhibit, where children learn about cause-and-effect by sending balls down chutes, shooting them up tubes, cranking them up a conveyor-belt, guiding them through a maze, and employing dozens of other contraptions designed to stimulate the imagination.

Older children will love the MindScape technology studio area. Recommended for 8 and up (although Josephine had fun here as young as 4), computers loaded with educational, child-friendly games and software stand ready for little fingers, but the real hits are the virtual reality games (when the museum isn't crowded, I've been known to work up a real sweat myself) and the real sound booth, complete with keyboard, guitar, drums, and vocals.

The grocery store is a blast for younger kids, while older children love to put on performances in the theater. The non-thespian child can have just as much fun controlling the lighting and sound effects. There's a Mexican restaurant, a global village, a sailboat, a fire truck, a Metro bus, a story area (call for storytelling schedule), and dozens of other exhibits.

The museum also has fascinating special exhibits that change regularly.

Keep in mind that with some 22,000 square feet of exhibit space, it is very easy for children to get separated from parents. On weekends when it is particularly crowded (we try to go during the week), panicky parents chasing toddlers is a common sight. For older kids, it's advisable to designate a meeting point and time. For a break from chasing your toddler, you might want to try out Discovery Bay . . .

Discovery Bay is an area exclusively for infants and toddlers up to 2 1/2 to explore without the disruptions and distractions that older kids can create. It's a cozy, well-padded, self-contained area with an aquarium, slide, books, and several "under sea" themed activities.

The Children's Museum also offers arts and crafts opportunities in its studio spaces. Call in advance for a schedule.

The bathrooms have fixtures scaled for both adults and children.

Downtown

Pacific Science Center

Southwest corner of Seattle Center grounds
General – (206) 443-2001
IMAX – (206) 443-IMAX
Laser – (206) 443-2850
www.pacsci.org

courtesy Erin Hogan

At Pacific Science Center's Body Works exhibit, visitors of all sizes learn about themselves.

Young children will have fun here, but this is really the venue for children who have outgrown the Children's Museum (6+). You can easily spend an entire day exploring both the temporary and permanent exhibits.

Probably the most popular of the science center's permanent exhibits are its seven roaring, robotic Mesozoic Era dinosaurs, presented in a naturalistic setting, which includes – to the terror of some smaller kids – a T-Rex.

We love the butterfly house (which you get to by passing through the Insect Village) with its dozens of beautiful varieties. There are always chrysalises (I grew up calling them "cocoons," but I've since been corrected by a number of scientifically-correct preschoolers) in various stages of development. It's sometimes hard to convince children to slow down, but the reward for a few minutes of quiet contemplation may be that you are landed upon by one of these exotic tropical specimens. Take the time to look closely into the foliage – the most stunning creatures aren't always on the wing!

The Puget Sound exhibit is a wonder for older, more scientifically minded youths, with its scale model of the sound, which allows you to examine the tides and currents by releasing dyes into the water. The saltwater tide pool allows children to see and touch a variety of the sound's indigenous creatures.

Children with the performance bug will love seeing themselves on TV posing as a guest weather forecaster, while the small animal exhibit (guinea pigs, snakes, mole-rats, and others) will attract your budding naturalist. Energetic kids will get to work off a bit of the excess in the Body Works exhibit where they are encouraged to test their reaction time

Pacific Science Center

Cost: Adults $8, seniors $5.50, junior (3-13) $5.50, under 3 free. IMAX and laser shows are extra and can be purchased as part of package deals. Call or check the website for details.

Hours: School year – Mon.-Fri. 10 a.m.-5 p.m.; Sat.-Sun. 10 a.m. - 6 p.m.; Summer – Daily, 10 a.m. - 6 p.m.; Closed Thanksgiving and Christmas.

Downtown

or check how many calories they can burn on the stationary bicycles. The Tech Zone features robots that play tic-tac-toe, virtual reality sports challenges (really fun for children over about 6), and an opportunity to create computer art.

The outdoor exhibits include water cannons, a two-ton granite ball you can spin with your bare hands, and, for adventurous older kids, a high rail bicycle that balances on a one-inch wide rail positioned 15 feet above the ground.

Young visitors play tic-tac-toe against a ten-foot tall robot in Pacific Science Center's 'Tech Zone'.

Most of the exhibits are beyond the capabilities and understanding of toddlers. When our daughter was younger, we spent most of our science center time in the special toddler area with its large water stream table, climbing and sliding toys, blocks and bubble station. If you're eager to try out some of the other exhibits yourself, being cooped up here with your children will be a frustrating experience (because they won't want to leave), but if you're ready to take a load off, it's a blessing.

The exhibits, however, are only a part of the science center experience. There is a cozy planetarium with live, interactive presentations, two IMAX theaters (additional cost), science demonstrations, laser shows (additional cost; family matinees; rock 'n' roll shows in the evening), and a cafeteria.

The science center also offers educational programs and camps for all ages, both at the center and "off-campus," including a very cool "Preschool Prowl" through a blueberry farm and a wetland. Call (206) 443-2925 for information about these and other educational programs.

Finally, the Pacific Science Center offers educational "babysitting" programs featuring trained docents at very reasonable rates. Call for details.

Downtown

Experience Music Project

East of the Space Needle on the Seattle Center Campus
(206) 367-5483
www.experience.org

What is that? The latest major addition to Seattle Center is housed in this incredible building designed by world-renowned architect Frank O. Gehry, which is unlike any building you've ever seen. Variously described as a "blob," a giant, anatomically correct human heart, an abomination, and a revelation, this interactive music museum is the brainchild of Microsoft co-founder and billionaire Paul Allen, whose idea for a museum dedicated to the life and art of Seattle-born guitarist Jimi Hendrix, exploded into this unique collection of state-of-the-art technology and world-class collection of pop music artifacts.

They try hard, but you'll likely be wasting your money and time taking children under 7 or 8, who probably haven't yet developed the skills, interest, or patience to enjoy the exhibits. By the same token, teenagers and savvy adolescents might well consider this to be the highlight of their trip to Seattle.

At the core of EMP's mission is the exploration and celebration of musical diversity, with an emphasis on blues, jazz, hip-hop, funk, punk, country, and rock 'n' roll.

The Roots and Branches exhibit, anchored by German artist Trimpin's sculpture, takes you on an audio-visual exploration of the roots of American popular music. More than 500 musical instruments and 30 computers were used to create the sculpture. The Guitar Gallery, featuring 55 guitars that "changed the world," gets rave reviews from pop music fans. The Northwest Passage exhibit takes a look at the Pacific Northwest music scene, from jazz and R&B, through the garage sounds of the "Louie Louie" era to heavy metal, "grunge," and right up to the independent sounds of today's music scene. The Hendrix Gallery focuses on the music and legacy of Jimi Hendrix, while the Milestones area contains a series of interconnected exhibits celebrating the independent spirit of rock 'n' roll.

The Sound Lab is where it all comes together, allowing you to move from the audience and onto the stage where you can play the guitars, bang on the drums, mix a record album, or perform for an audience of thousands. This is the busiest part of the museum – during the summer and on weekends, be prepared to wait for a chance to try the more popular interactive exhibits.

> **Experience Music Project**
>
> Cost: Adults $19.95, seniors $15.95, youth (13-17) $15.95, children (7-12) $14.95, under 7 free.
>
> Hours: Sun.-Thurs., 10 a.m. - 5 p.m.; Fri.-Sat., 10 a.m. - 9 p.m. Turntable Restaurant opens at 11 a.m. (does not require EMP admission).

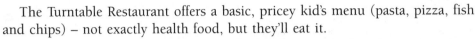

Downtown

The Turntable Restaurant offers a basic, pricey kid's menu (pasta, pizza, fish and chips) – not exactly health food, but they'll eat it.

EMP offers an ever-changing array of special events and performances, an arts camp for children 7-12, and other educational opportunities, both at EMP and other venues. Call for details.

I would highly recommend visiting the EMP's excellent website prior to visiting, but don't expect anyone to answer your emails.

International Fountain

Seattle Center Campus
(206) 684-7200

In warm weather, we sometimes come to Seattle Center just to play in the International Fountain. The silver dome, set down in a large bowl, spouts water from its dozens of nozzles, alternating between majestic heights and meager drizzles. Children of all ages – fully clothed and in bathing suits – run in and out of the shower, shrieking.

International Fountain

Cost: Free

Hours: Daily, 11 a.m. - 11 p.m.

Just another gorgeous day at the fountain!

courtesy Seattle Center

One of the most popular "left-overs" from the World's Fair, the fountain is surrounded by open space and lawn, which makes it a popular place for a picnic.

During the winter, the fountain is dramatically and colorfully lit as part of the Winterfest celebration.

Downtown

Seattle Center House

Seattle Center campus
(206) 684-7200

The Center House is the permanent home to inexpensive restaurants, confectioners, retailers, a small children's play area (upstairs), and The Children's Museum (downstairs; see above). It is also the temporary home to a variety of community events, celebrations, and performances throughout the year.

Seattle Center House
Cost: Free
Hours: Sun.-Thurs. 11 a.m. - 6 p.m., Fri.-Sat. 11 a.m. - 8 p.m.

A useful, functional facility, we usually eat lunch here after a visit to The Children's Museum. The food is nothing to write home about, but at least you have the option of Thai or Chinese while the kids munch pizza and hotdogs.

Often you will get free entertainment with your meal. For instance, Josephine enjoys watching the ballroom dancers who meet here on a regular basis.

Seattle Center Skate Park

Just across 5th Ave. N from the main Seattle Center campus
(206) 669-1297

Seattle Center Skate Park
Cost: Free
Hours: Daily, dawn to dusk.

If you have a skateboarder in tow, you'll likely want to check out this 8,900-square-foot, outdoor skate park. In-line skaters and skateboarders of all ages and skill levels are invited to take a spin on the snake run, the bowl, the quarter pipes, and the street grind.

Mostly, you will find teenagers here, although our friend Mike – a thirty-something father – is known to drop by for a skate. He tells me there is great, safe stroller parking inside the fence. If you hear kids shouting, "Way to go, old dude!" you'll know Mike is here.

Downtown

Seattle Center Monorail

**Seattle Center campus to Westlake Center
(5th Ave. and Pine; station is upstairs)
(206) 441-6038
www.seattlemonorail.com**

As far as Josephine is concerned, we could just ride the monorail back-and-forth all day. Another vestige of the 1962 World's Fair, the monorail leaves every 10 minutes, taking you to the heart of downtown in 2 minutes.

Try to get the seat by the driver.

Seattle Center Monorail

Fares (one-way): Adults $1.25, children (5-12) and seniors 50¢, under 5 free.

Hours: Mon.-Fri., 7:30 a.m. - 11 p.m.; Sat.-Sun., 9 a.m. - 11 p.m.

courtesy Seattle Center

Seattle's Historic Monorail

The Seattle Children's Theatre

**Just inside the west entrance to Seattle Center campus.
Administration: (206) 443-0807
Tickets: (206) 441-3322
Drama school: (206) 443-0807
www.sct.org**

courtesy Seattle Children's Theatre

Seattle Children's Theatre

The Seattle Children's Theatre is the West Coast's largest professional theatre for family audiences and annually performs for more than a quarter of a million people. Most of the productions are designed for children 8-years-old and up, although each season includes performances for younger audiences. The age-

Downtown

The Seattle Children's Theatre

Cost: Adults $21.50-$22.50, children/seniors $14.50-$15.50.

Hours: Call for show times.

You can see it in their eyes—theatre is fun!

recommendations are only there to give you an idea; it's up to you to know your own child. The Charlotte Martin Theatre does have a "quiet room" with a view of the stage for children who have trouble sitting still.

We've attended several performances over the years, enjoying ourselves immensely each time. This is real, professional theater for children, performed in a modern, comfortable setting. Unlike so many performances for children, you won't feel like you're suffering through anything. This is a treat – albeit a bit on the expensive side – for both kids and their parents. Group discounts and subscriptions are a couple of ways to reduce the cost.

Pricey snacks and meals are available, or you can eat at the Center House.

SCT offers excellent drama and acting classes for children in grades 3-12 as well as camps during school breaks. Call for more information.

Seattle International Children's Festival

Seattle Center campus
(206) 684-7338
www.seattleinternational.org

Seattle International Children's Festival

Cost: Call for prices.

Season/Hours: Mid-May. Call for specific hours and dates.

Each May, the Seattle Center grounds are given over to the Seattle International Children's Festival. Starting as a small arts event for children, this six-day annual event has grown into the largest performing arts festival for families in the United States. Artists from all over the world congregate here in a colorful, lively, entertaining, and educational celebration.

Downtown

Seattle Sonics and Storm

Key Arena on the west side of Seattle Center campus.
(206) 281-5800
1-800-4NBA-TIX (Sonic tickets); 206-217-WNBA (Storm tickets)
www.nba.com/sonics and www.wnba.com/storm

Seattle Sonics and Storm

Cost: $9-$110.

Season: Oct.-April (Sonics); May-August (Storm). Call or visit websites for schedule.

The NBA's Sonics (men) and the WNBA's Storm (women) are Seattle's professional basketball teams. Recently remodeled Key Arena is a bright, exciting place to take in a game. The Sonics are fun, but NBA players have notoriously foul-mouths, which you can often hear even up to the rafters. We're far more likely to attend Storm games, where the language is cleaner, the brand of basketball just as exciting, and the player attitudes something you might actually want your child to emulate.

Seattle Thunderbirds

Key Arena on the West side of Seattle Center campus
(206) 728-9121
www.seattle-thunderbirds.com

Lacking an NHL franchise, the Western Hockey League Seattle Thunderbirds are the best option for hockey fans. The players are 16-20 years old and the team plays a 72-game season between September and March. The Canadian Hockey League, comprised of the Western League and the Ontario and Quebec Leagues, provides more talent to the NHL and other professional leagues than any other source in the world.

Celebrating a goal!

T-Bird players and Cool Bird visit children and families at Ronald McDonald House.

Downtown

Pacific Northwest Ballet

Performances at the Opera House on the north side of Seattle Center campus
(206) 441-9411 (main desk)
(206) 441-2424 (box office)
www.pnb.org

Pacific Northwest Ballet

Cost: $15-$115

Season: August-January. Call or check website for schedule.

The Pacific Northwest Ballet is generally considered to be one of the top ballet companies in the U.S. While most of its performances are not appropriate for smaller children, the ballet fan in your family will be thrilled by these Kent Stowell and Francia Russell directed performances. Each season generally includes a mixture of modern and classical ballets, although the company specializes in the ballets of George Balancine.

PNB's annual performance of *The Nutcracker* is one of the highlights of our December holiday season. We've been taking our daughter since she was just over a year old with magical results. Actively promoted as a family event, a certain level of hubbub is tolerated, as are bathroom and lobby runs. PNB sells a video of their *Nutcracker* production, which we use to prepare our daughter for what to expect, although the cannon blast during the battle with the mice still startles her every year.

For other performances, you have to use your judgment. PNB welcomes children, but recommends that the decision to bring your young child be based upon the ballet being performed and the maturity of your child. We attended *The Sleeping Beauty*, for instance, when our daughter was four, and while it is some 3 hours long, she behaved appropriately and loved it.

Another option is to ask about student performances, which are highly entertaining with the added bonus of being more casual and far, far cheaper.

The PNB school (located just to the west of the Opera House) offers ballet classes for girls and boys from 5-years-old on up. Call (206) 441-2435 for information.

Downtown

The Waterfront

The non-industrial waterfront runs along Alaskan Way from Pier 48 at the foot of Main, north to (and including) Myrtle Edwards Park.

This is the most kitschy, touristy part of Seattle, a place where the only locals you're likely to run into are the ones who work there or are on an outing to the Seattle Aquarium. This doesn't mean that you won't want to visit – in fact, it's exactly this tourist orientation that makes it such a great place to take the kids. Nearly every pier is home to one or more attractions, tours, views, and treats. It's also a place from which to take-off for day-trips around and about the Puget Sound.

Our favorite way to "do" the waterfront is to park at one end, walk and explore until we're tired, then hop the waterfront trolley back to the car.

> **The Waterfront**
>
> Directions: From I-5 north or south, follow signs to "Ferries" (exits 164B from I-5 N and 164 from I-5 S). Turn right on 4th Ave. S, then right on South Royal Brougham Way. Turn right on Alaskan Way. Metered parking under the viaduct and pay lots at the south end of Alaskan Way. Metered parking at Myrtle Edwards Park at the north end.

Things to Do

Pier 48

Alaskan Way at the foot of Main Street

> **Pier 48**
>
> Cost: Free

Children enjoy peering through the periscopes on the waterfront side of the pier, which provides close-up perspectives of Elliott Bay. You will also find a nice little display of the harbor's history.

courtesy Nick Gunderson

Seattle's waterfront is always a treat.

Downtown

Coleman Dock and Riding Ferries

Alaskan Way at the foot of Marion Street (Pier 58)
(206) 464-6400
www.wsdot.wa.gov/ferries/index.cfm

Even if you don't have the time for a ferry ride, you'll still want to walk out to the end of Pier 52 and watch the ferries load and unload. A ubiquitous part of the scenery and a vital piece of the state's highway system, thousands of travelers and commuters ride these ferries every day. The Washington State Ferry System is the largest in the United States, serving eight counties in Washington and the Province of British Columbia in Canada, carrying more than 26 million people each year. The ferry "Tacoma" alone, which travels the Bainbridge Island run, can handle 2,500 passengers per trip.

Of course, it's much more fun to ride than to watch. We often pack a picnic lunch and make an afternoon of a trip to Bainbridge Island (see chapter 5) and back, generally not even bothering to disembark, a round-trip of approximately 1-1/2 hours. Ferries sail between 6:20 a.m. and 1:30 a.m. If you choose the Bremerton ferry, double the sailing time. There is no better view of the Seattle skyline than from the deck of a ferry, so don't forget to take a camera. You'll also want to pack jackets even on warm summer days, as it can be windy on the outside decks.

Seagulls follow your path and are always happy to snap up any breadcrumbs or French fries that may happen to fall overboard.

You don't have to pack a lunch. The ferry "galleys" generally serve breakfast, lunch, and dinner during peak hours. You will also find shakes, wine, beer, and on some routes, espresso.

My only complaint about riding the ferry is that my daughter has occasionally spent the entire trip at the steering wheel of one of the on-board video games (no, I don't insert coins, but that doesn't stop her).

> **Coleman Dock and Riding Ferries**
>
> Cost: Free to watch. Walk-on round-trip fares to Bainbridge Island or Bremerton: Adults $4.50, children $3.20 (under 5 free), seniors $2.20. Vehicles are $8 from 2nd Sun. in Oct. through the 2nd Sat. in May; and $10 from the 2nd Sun. in May through 2nd Sat. in Oct. Fares subject to change. For the latest rate and schedule information, call or check online.

Downtown

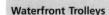

Waterfront Trolleys

Alaskan Way
(206) 553-3000
http://transit.metrokc.gov

Waterfront Trolleys

Cost: Adults $1.00 or $1.25 (depending on time of day), children 50 cents (under 5 ride free). Ask the driver for a "transfer" and your pass will be good for 90 minutes of sightseeing. Fares subject to change; phone for the latest fare and schedule information.

There are few things our daughter loves more than a ride on the streetcar (especially if it ends up at the Old Spaghetti Factory (see below). Metro's Waterfront Streetcar provides trolley access to the International District, Pioneer Square, and the full length of Seattle's non-industrial waterfront. Service is provided on meticulously maintained 1927 Australian streetcars brought from Melbourne beginning in 1982. The coaches feature Tasmanian mahogany and white ash woodwork, capturing the elegance of travel in a bygone era. Accommodating 52 seated and 40 standing passengers, the streetcars – and stations – are fully accessible for disabled riders. The Streetcar runs approximately every 20 minutes, seven days a week. You may get on and off at any stop.

The conductors are friendly and eager to answer your questions.

Argosy Cruises

Alaskan Way at the foot of Spring St. (Pier 55 & 56)
(206) 623-4252
www.argosycruises.com

Argosy Cruises

Cost: Harbor Cruise – Adults $16.00, children ages 4-12 $10.00, seniors/groups (8 or more) $14.00

Locks Cruise – Adults $30.00, children ages 4-12 $16.00, seniors/groups (8 or more) $28.00

The ferry is cheaper, but Argosy's Harbor Cruise is a one-hour narrated adventure around Elliott Bay and the Seattle Harbor, including a dramatic venture under the Port of Seattle cranes that line the Duwamish Waterway. The longer (2 1/2 hour) Locks Cruise is even more fascinating, taking you from Elliott Bay, through the ever-interesting Hiram Chittenden Locks and into Lake Union, where you will have a waterside view of the funky houseboat community made famous by the movie "Sleepless in Seattle."

This is one of the many Seattle attractions that those of us who live here never enjoy except when guests are visiting from out of town. I'm always embarrassed and amazed at how much I didn't know about my hometown. The cruises run year-round, rain or shine. Argosy recommends reservations, especially during the summer months, but walk-ups are welcome when space is available.

Argosy can also arrange private cruises on one of their 13 vessels for groups from 10 to 800. If you have a teenager's birthday party to plan, you might want to consider this. Dinner cruises are also available, but you'll need a sitter for the kids.

Cruise boat coming
in to port

Downtown

Seattle IMAX Dome Theatre

Pier 59 at the foot of Pike Place Market
(206) 622-1868
www.seattleimaxdome.com

> **Seattle IMAX Dome Theatre**
>
> Cost: Adults $7, seniors $6.50, children $6, under 5 free.
>
> Showtimes: 10 a.m. - 7 p.m. (call for current schedule)

Just so you know, children under 5 are free, but the gigantic images and the "Hexophonic sound system" will scare the daylights out of some of them, especially if you're there for the spectacular film about the eruption of Mount St. Helens in 1980. Most of the movies here are educational and nature films on steroids. If you're going to spend an afternoon at the movies, you really can't do better than this for you or your children – they'll be entertained and might even learn something. Call first for movies and show times.

Fire Station 5

925 Alaskan Way
Waterfront
Battalion 2
(206) 386-1400
www.ci.seattle.wa.us/fire/home.htm

Located between the ferry terminal and Ivar's Fish Bar, Fire Station 5 is home to Engine 4, the "Chief Seattle" fireboat. This white and black vessel with red trim and "water cannons" is a favorite. You can get a view of it up close at its dock, but if you are really lucky, it will be out on the Sound, blasting those cannons skyward in a show of firefighting prowess, with a pumping capacity of 7,500 gallons per minute.

> **Fire Station 5**
>
> Cost: Free
>
> Hours: Call to schedule tour

Tours of the station can be arranged by calling the number listed above, although be forewarned that children under 5 are not permitted until they have completed a fire safety curriculum (call 206-386-1338 to order the curriculum). Tours last about 20 minutes, must be scheduled at least 7 days in advance, and may be scheduled for between the hours of 9 a.m. and 11:30 a.m. and 1 p.m. and 4 p.m., Monday-Saturday. Keep in mind that the fire station remains "in-service" during tours, so you may be left behind if firefighters are called on to respond to an emergency. Also, birthday party groups are welcome, but party festivities (including cake and ice cream) are not allowed in the station.

Downtown

Seattle Aquarium

1483 Alaskan Way (Pier 59)
(206) 386-4300
www.seattleaquarium.org

The otters are our favorite, followed closely by the seals – both of which can be viewed from above or below. We pretend to be afraid of the sharks, but the sight of the giant Pacific octopus climbing the glass, tentacles outward, causes genuine anxiety. This is one of those "tourist attractions" to which locals come in equal, if not greater, numbers. For one thing, it is among the best rainy day places for children in the city – invariably we run into someone we know. Keep a sharp eye on your toddlers because it's easy to get lost in this mazy, darkened wonderland of Pacific Northwest sea life. The underwater dome is popular as are the hands-on "pools" where visitors can handle starfish, anemones, and other tidal creatures.

courtesy Seattle Aquarium

Inside the Aquarium.

Seattle Aquarium

Cost: Adults $9.50, senior/handicapped $8.50, youth (6-18) $6.75, child (3-5) $4.75, under 3 free. (The Aquarium offers "combination" discounts for those interested in buying tickets for the Aquarium in conjunction with other venues, such as the Woodland Park Zoo, Seattle IMAX Dome, and the Odyssey Maritime Discovery Center. Call 386-4330 for additional information about combination and King County resident discounts.)

Season/Hours:
Day after Labor Day - Memorial Day, 10 a.m. - 5 p.m.; Day after Memorial Day - Labor Day, 9:30 a.m. - 7 p.m.

If you are lucky, or if you do some initial phone work, you can watch the divers feed the fish in the dome aquarium or watch the marine mammals enjoy their fish dinners. There is a small aquarium-themed play area for your youngest kids and opportunities for older children to dig more deeply into the areas that interest them.

The Aquarium also offers a number of trips and adventures that take place outside the facility, such as Orca watching excursions, guided kayaking trips, and various educational cruises (both one-day and longer). Aquarium Beach Naturalists are also on hand at South Alki, Golden Gardens, Carkeek Park, Lincoln Park, Richmond Beach, Des Moines, and Seahurst at low tides. Call (206) 386-4353 for more details and/or to sign-up.

The Aquarium is also available for private parties.

Downtown

Tillicum Village Cruise

Pier 55 at the foot of Spring Street
1-800-426-1205
www.tillicumvillage.com

Tillicum Village Cruise

Cost: Adults $65, senior $59, child (5-12) $25, under 5 free.

Schedule: Year-round. Oct.-April, weekends only, May-Sept., daily. Call ahead as schedule varies. Reservations recommended.

This 4-hour, 8-mile narrated excursion takes you across Puget Sound to Blake Island Marine State Park and includes, upon your arrival, a delicious barbequed salmon dinner prepared using the traditional Northwest Coast Native American method, a half-hour performance by the Tillicum Village dancers, which touches on the mythology and customs of various Northwest tribes, and an opportunity to explore the beach and forest trails, as well as watch the village artisans work, before heading back to Seattle.

While the educational aspect is exactly the sort of homogenized simplification that Native Americans often complain about, there is no denying that this is a fun, memorable experience. It's a long day, however, and will tax toddlers.

Odyssey Marine Discovery Center

Pier 66, 2205 Alaskan Way
(206) 374-4000
www.ody.org

Odyssey Marine Discovery Center

Cost: Adults $6.75, seniors 62+ $4.50, students 5 to 18 $4.50. Children 4 and under, no charge.

Hours: May 15 - Sept. 15 – Mon.-Sat. 10 a.m. - 5 p.m.; Sun. Noon - 5 p.m.; Sept. 16 - May 14 – Tues. - Sat. 10 a.m. - 5 p.m.; Sun. Noon - 5 pm. Closed Mondays, Thanksgiving, Christmas, New Year's Day, Martin Luther King Day, and President's Day.

Located in the relatively new Bell Street Pier convention center, this is one of the best "undiscovered" attractions in all of Seattle. Here is a completely interactive experience that will entertain your children while they learn about the Puget Sound, its environment, and the local marine economy. Your kids will love the kayak journey, which allows visitors to sit in a full-sized kayak and paddle through a virtual Skagit or Elliott Bay. Or how about the challenging Port of Seattle crane exhibit, which lets you load or unload a virtual container vessel? Smaller kids get a kick out of the marine playscape, where they can wear lifejackets, operate a fish conveyer, skipper a skiff, or plot a course. You can captain a container vessel, use real radar equipment to track actual marine traffic on Puget Sound, and dozens of other fun things

Both the best and worst thing about Odyssey is that people still haven't discovered it. We've often been the only ones there, which means no waiting for the more popular attractions, but also leaves you feeling a little lonesome.

Downtown

Bell Street Pier and Bell Harbor Marina

2203 Alaskan Way (Pier 66)
(206) 441-6666

Home to the Odyssey Maritime Discovery Center (see above), the Anthony's restaurants (see below) and the Bell Harbor Marina, you will also find public plazas with benches and telescopes, a cute kid's wading pool (which is rarely in use), and cruise ship births.

If you happen to be arriving in Seattle by boat, the Bell Harbor Marina offers short-term moorage for recreational vessels ranging from 30 to 100 feet. Reservations are accepted for stays of longer than 24 hours. Water hook-ups, 24-hour staffing and security, showers, electricity, and other services make this quite a comfy place to stay. Call (206) 615-3952 or email **bhm@portseattle.org** for more information.

Waterfront Park

1301 Alaskan Way (Pier 58)

This is essentially a viewpoint park, featuring a fountain, public fishing, a few picnic tables, and a bizarre statue of Christopher Columbus. Not a bad place to take your sack lunch on a sunny day, but be prepared to be hit-up for spare change.

There are restrooms, but they aren't of the more pleasant sort. You'll be happier with the private facilities on Pier 59. Also, the railings around the pier are too far apart. Children can easily get their heads through, which means their bodies can follow – keep an eye out!

Bay Pavilion

1301 Alaskan Way (Pier 57)
(206) 623-8600
www.p57.com

The Bay Pavilion is where you will rub shoulders with all the other tourists lured in by the various shops hawking souvenirs, t-shirts, fudge, and saltwater taffy. There are also a couple of unspectacular seafood restaurants here. I've never eaten here, nor have I known anyone who has confessed to doing so.

Aside from the candy, the main attraction for your children will be the indoor, old-time wooden horse carousel.

A number of painted, woodcarvings decorate the pavilion. Does anyone besides me think the one by the carousel looks like Stockard Channing?

Downtown

Victoria Clipper

Clipper Navigation, Inc.
2701 Alaskan Way, Pier 69
(206) 448-5000 or 1-800-888-2535
www.clippervacations.com

Victoria Clipper

Cost: Varies, call or check the website for fares to your desired destination(s).

Schedule: Subject to change, call or check the website.

Victoria, British Columbia (which is in Canada) is a charming place with an old-Europe feel about it. The Victoria Clipper is a popular way to get there. This speedy passenger-only boat can get you to Victoria Island in 2 hours, which on the surface seems faster than driving, but be forewarned that if you aren't checked-in at least an hour before departure, you can lose your seats, which of course makes the "journey" more like 3 to 4 hours – a long-haul for youngsters. You will want to spend at least one night in Victoria to make the trip worthwhile, although a whole weekend is better.

The Clipper can also take you to the San Juan Islands.

Your best bet might be to book one of Clipper Vacations' 15 package deals, which include trips to Vancouver, Portland, and Whistler, with accommodations included.

Here's the best part: if you book at least 7 days in advance, children 11 and under, travel free (with some exceptions).

Port of Seattle Headquarters

2711 Alaskan Way (Pier 69)
(206) 728-3000
www.portseattle.org

Port of Seattle Headquarters

Cost: Free

Hours: 9 a.m. - 5 p.m.

The Port of Seattle is one of the most important institutions in our region, governing everything to do with both recreational and commercial shipping and Sea-Tac International Airport.

This refurbished, historic pier now serves as port headquarters. The 3-story building houses offices of the Port Commission, Commission Chambers, Executive, Legal, Seaport, and other port support services. First floor tenants include Portside Cafe, Clipper Navigation, and Seafloor Surveys. A self-guided walking tour is available from the receptionist. An interpretive center in the lobby offers a glimpse of the inner workings of the harbor.

Other highlights include artworks by eight Northwest artists uniquely integrated into the design of the building, plus a collection of Asian art presented to the Port by visiting delegations, visitors and customers.

I wouldn't expect my toddler to enjoy this, but adolescents and teens with a certain amount of curiosity about maritime or economic themes will be interested.

Downtown

Myrtle Edwards Park/Elliott Bay Park

Entrance is just north of Pier 70

This 3.7-acre slip of land along the shores of Elliott Bay is barely wide enough to accommodate the 1.25 mile walking and cycling trails; it has no playground equipment, and no restrooms. What it does have are incredible views of the bay, the Olympic Mountains, and Mt. Rainier, a busy train track along its eastern boundary (which entertains the little ones), a grain terminal from which giant cargo vessels are loaded with the products of Eastern Washington, and an exercise course.

The park continues northward along the waterfront about a mile farther under the name Elliott Bay Park, which is managed by the Port of Seattle. Elliott Bay Park features a 400-foot fishing pier, restrooms, a tackle shop, and snacks.

This is a great urban hike for those in quest of a little family exercise.

I love to ride my bike here (the bike trail continues through both parks, then connects to additional trails that take you to Magnolia and beyond) when the sun is shining, but I like it even better in my rain gear. It's not for the faint of heart, but older kids might enjoy the experience of being pelted by rain and buffeted by the winds, especially if the trip ends with a big bowl of hot clam chowder at one of the waterfront restaurants.

**Myrtle Edwards Park/
Elliott Bay Park**

Cost: Free

Downtown

Elliott Bay Water Taxi

Pier 54
(206) 553-3000
www.metrokc.gov

Elliott Bay Water Taxi

Cost: $2; under 5 ride for free.

Hours: Mon.-Thurs., 6:45 a.m. - 7 p.m.; Fri., 6:45 a.m. - 10:30 p.m.; Sat.-Sun., 8:30 a.m. - 10:30 p.m.

The cheapest way to get out on the water. Although its primary function is to ferry commuters, we like taking the round-trip to West Seattle's Seacrest Park just for fun. We've ordinarily taken the trip from the Seattle side, but many West Seattle residents hop the "taxi," which lands at Pier 54 on the waterfront, for quick, stress-free visits to downtown and Pike Place Market.

Let's Go Sailing

Pier 54
(206) 624-3931

Let's Go Sailing

Cost: $23-$38.

Schedule: May 1-Oct. 15—11 a.m., 1:30 p.m., 4 p.m. and sunset.

This is the life! A 70-foot sailboat with your own captain. Or, if you wish, you can take the helm. Choose from a 1 or a 2 hour tour. Take your own food if there's a chance you'll get hungry. Call first to make sure lifejackets are available in your children's sizes.

Downtown

Places to Eat

Ivar's Fish Bar and Original Acres of Clams Restaurant

Pier 54, just south of the Coleman ferry terminal
(206) 624-6852
www.ivars.net

This Seattle institution is regularly ranked by residents as having the best seafood, fish 'n chips, and chowder in the area. It's a sentimental choice (in my humble opinion), based more on an admiration for the chain's (30 restaurants throughout Washington and Oregon) beloved founder Ivar Haglund (1905-1985) who opened the place in 1938 and went on to become a local legend. His famous, good-natured admonition to "Keep Clam," his clam-eating contests, sing-alongs, and octopus-wrestling helped make Ivar's one of the area's most popular family restaurants.

You have two choices here. The fish bar is, naturally, less expensive and the menu is

courtesy Ivar's Fish Bar

Ivar Haglund (1905-1985), local legend!

limited, but this is the only way you will get to sit outside to enjoy the most quintessential of all Ivar's attractions – feeding the seagulls. Ivar himself believed so strongly in this activity that you will find a statue of him on the sidewalk in front of the place doing just that. An enclosed, heated outdoor eating area is available as is outdoor seating along the pier railing. You will likely need an extra order of fries for the dozens of seagulls that clog the water below and circle overhead. It's a blast to watch these scavengers snatch your offering in mid-air. I must warn you, however, that the gulls can be incredibly aggressive – one recently snuck up behind Josephine as she was tossing fries and nearly snatched the food right from her hand. I've seen a number of small children reduced to tears and more than one dining party has been harassed to the point of retreating to the enclosed area to finish in peace. That said, this is my daughter's favorite waterfront activity.

The way we enjoy Ivar's is to take choice number two, and duck into the restaurant itself. The same food is obviously a little more expensive, but the menu is more extensive, and you can watch the seagulls (ask for a window table) without being dive-bombed. A children's menu is available, which includes several non-seafood items. We then fill up a doggy bag with our leftovers to feed the gulls afterward.

Downtown

Elliott's Oyster House

1201 Alaskan Way (Pier 56)
(206) 623-4340

This is a notch above Ivar's in terms of quality and price. It's been renovated recently and has outdoor seating during summer months. It's a more "adult" restaurant than some of the others on the waterfront, but the service is prompt enough and the menu variety sufficient to satisfy all but the most restless and/or picky.

Anthony's at Pier 66

2201 Alaskan Way (Pier 66)
(206) 448-6688
www.anthonys.com/pierdiner.htm#Pier 66

This is actually three excellent seafood restaurants in one: Anthony's Pier 66 (fine-dining; upstairs), Anthony's Bell Street Diner (mid-scale; table service), and Anthony's Fish Bar (casual; walk-up). The diner and fish bar are the most appropriate for families with young children and both have outdoor seating available in the summer. You'll enjoy great seafood along with many other choices, prompt service, and a nice view.

Hotel Edgewater

2411 Alaskan Way (Pier 67)
(206) 728-7000 or (800) 624-0670
www.noblehousehotels.com/edgewater

Seattle's only waterfront hotel. I've included it here, because this hotel restaurant has the best view of any on the waterfront. The building, perched out over the water, has sweeping views of Elliott Bay and Olympic Mountains.

We like to come here for brunch.

Downtown

The Old Spaghetti Factory

2801 Elliott Ave.
(206) 441-7724
www.osf.com

Located across the railroad tracks at the extreme north end of the non-industrial waterfront, The Old Spaghetti Factory is what a family restaurant should be. It's big, noisy, and colorfully decorated, including an old train car in which to dine (although you'll likely have to wait for a table in it). The service is remarkably fast, the prices are low, and the food surprisingly good. The kid's dinner is a particularly good deal including pasta, applesauce, bread, a drink, and dessert for under $4. Children receive a free activity book to work on, although the service is so fast they don't really have the time to enjoy it!

On weekends, you'll have to wait for a table during peak dinner hours (we try to get there by 5:45 to avoid waiting).

Red Robin Burger and Spirits

Pier 55
(206) 623-1942

Red Robin is a locally-based chain known primarily for its "gourmet" burgers. It's a loud, busy place with a reasonably-priced children's menu offering items of both the burger and non-burger variety, along with a "bottomless" fries policy, which means you don't need to steal them from your child's plate.

Places to Shop

Ye Olde Curiosity Shop

1001 Alaskan Way - Pier 54 (next door to Ivar's)
(206) 682-5844
www.yeoldecuriosityshop.com

Whenever we're in the mood for a shrunken head, a three-tailed pig, or just want to say "hi" to Sylvester the Mummy (or his companion Sylvia), this is where we come. Ye Olde Curiosity Shop has been at this location for over 100 years, opening its doors in 1899 and remaining in the hands of the same family for four generations. It's a museum of oddities, (including real shrunken heads – not for sale), a Native American art gallery, and curiosity-novelty-gift-collectables shop rolled into one. You may buy your own shrunken head (made of goat's skin or rubber).

This store may be a bit creepy for some children, but you'll have a hard time dragging your older kids away.

Downtown

Belltown

Belltown is bordered by Virginia Street to the south, Broad Street to the north, 1st Avenue to the west, and 5th Avenue to the east.

Belltown

Directions: From I-5 north, take the Olive/Denny exit, turn left onto Denny Way, then left onto Stewart. Follow Stewart to 1st Avenue and turn right. Drive one block to Virginia and you are at the most southeastern corner of Belltown. From I-5 south, take the Stewart Street exit, continue on Stewart as directed above.

Belltown is the more common appellation given to the downtown neighborhood officially called the Denny Regrade. The last decade has seen Belltown blossom into one of Seattle's hottest neighborhoods. Dozens of new and remodeled condominiums, restaurants, and funky retail shops – especially along 1st Avenue – have transformed this once artsy, somewhat dangerous neighborhood into a mecca for hip, young singles. That being the case, this is not the most family-oriented neighborhood, although that seems to be changing slightly as more and more of these young urbanites have babies.

The main thing to do in Belltown is eat, and I'm here to tell you that the eating is good. Many of Seattle's top restaurants are here (*Lamprea, The Flying Fish, Fandango, Cascadia, El Gaucho,* to name but a few), but these are best saved for babysitter nights. Fortunately, Belltown is also home to some of our favorite casual establishments. As is true in any neighborhood in the process of transformation, the specific roster of restaurants is ever-changing as little mom-and-pop places open and close almost daily.

Things to Do

Belltown P-Patch

Elliott Ave. and Vine St.
(206) 684-0264

This city-owned community garden was established in 1994 to give downtown residents a patch of land upon which to grow gardens. It's a funky, little oasis that charms smaller children. It only takes a few minutes for an adult to traverse its pathways, but with a toddler in charge, there is at least an hour's worth of discovery here.

Downtown

Regrade Park
3rd Ave. and Bell St.

This tiny urban park has playground equipment and a basketball hoop, but don't let that fool you. This is not a place for children. The park tends to be populated most hours of the day and night by street alcoholics and other nefarious types. Keep on walking.

Places to Eat

Zeek's Pizza
419 Denny Way
(206) 285-TOGO
www.zeekspizza.com

Situated in a location in no-man's land between Belltown and Seattle Center, this Zeek's Pizza restaurant is one of a local chain serving some of Seattle's best and most bizarre pizza. Josephine sticks with cheese pizza, but your older children might be bold enough to try the "Frog Belly Green" (olive and pesto) or "Thai One On" (peanut sauce, chicken, bean sprouts, etc.). The gigantic salads are winners.

The staff here, as with all the Zeek's, are young, friendly, and will make your children laugh.

Crocodile Café
2200 2nd Ave.
(206) 441-5611

I've included the Crocodile Café for those with teenage pop music lovers. If there is a birthplace of the music that the world came to know as "grunge" or the "Seattle sound," this is it. Nirvana, Mudhoney, and the rest of those 1990s acts put this place on the map, and it continues to be the venue of choice for up-and-coming acts. Owned by the wife of R.E.M. bandmember Peter Buck, the Crocodile is no place for children at night, but by day, the front room is a solid, funky restaurant where those with sharp eyes and a finger on the pulse can often spot local musicians lunching on soup and sandwiches. You shouldn't have trouble finding something to satisfy the picky pallet. We like the Crocodile for breakfast where we stuff ourselves with giant bowls of Oatmeal with Cinnamon and Apples – try it, you won't have to eat again until dinner!

Downtown

Sit and Spin
2219 4th Ave
(206) 441-9484

Like the Crocodile Café, Sit and Spin is a music venue at night, but during the day, it's a funky laundromat and lunch counter with an emphasis on vegetarian food. Your kids will find something on the menu they will like, and the selection of board games should keep older ones occupied. You might even get a load of laundry done.

Lake Union

Lake Union is as far from Golden Pond as a body of water can get. While it is still in transition from its boat-building/servicing past, what industrial evidence you see is largely historical remnants. While still used for commercial purposes, the lake is the backyard to hundreds of houseboats and dozens of restaurants. Float planes regularly take-off and land in its waters, and recreational boaters ply the waters.

Our main focus here is on the east and southern sides of the lake (the northern shore is discussed in connection with Fremont and Wallingford, and the west side has very limited public access).

Lake Union

Directions: From I-5 north or south, take the Mercer St. exit (#167 – from I-5 north, it is a left-hand exit). Bear right onto Fairview Ave. N Lake Union will be directly in front of you. From this point follow directions to specific attractions as noted below.

Downtown

Things to Do

Center for Wooden Boats

1010 Valley St.
(206) 382-2628
www.cwb.org

Featuring some 75 vintage (and some replica) wooden sailing and rowing vessels in its collection which floats in its own cozy harbor, the center was founded in the interest of keeping alive the heritage of wooden boats (as opposed to the modern fiberglass models). You will also often find new vessels in the process of being built and older ones being restored to their former glory. During a recent visit, for example, a three-masted, late 1800s logging vessel was waiting for some tender, loving care.

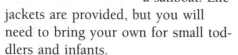

Boathouse

The coolest part is that you can actually rent many of these boats to take out onto Lake Union, where you can take-in one of the very best Seattle skyline views. Rental rates range from $10-37.50, and you will need to prove you can handle a sailboat. Life jackets are provided, but you will need to bring your own for small toddlers and infants.

Free half-hour sails on classic boats take place every Sunday at 2 p.m. Call to make sure weather permits.

The center offers both sailing lessons and boatbuilding classes for all ages, including a 5-day live-aboard sailing adventure for children 14-18, and summer camps for children 12-18. Call for details.

A vintage boat-ride at the Center for Wooden Boats

Downtown

"Sleepless in Seattle" Houseboats

East side of Lake Union

At the end of E Newton St., you will find the almost-not-there-at-all Terry Pettus Park, where you can have a picnic and get a good look at the houseboats moored there. You can also see the houseboats by walking northward along Fairview. At E Lynn St., you will find another diminutive park – Lynn Street Park – which will give you another perspective on these unique homes.

**"Sleepless in Seattle"
Houseboats**

Directions: (See directions to Lake Union.) From Fairview Ave. N, turn right onto Eastlake Ave., then continue to E Newton St. and turn left. At the end of the street (where it meets Fairview Ave. E), look for free on-street parking. Only residents may park on the west side of Fairview after 6 p.m. This is the southern end of the Lake Union houseboat community.

This is just a small remnant of what was once Seattle's answer to low-income housing. No longer inexpensive, some original homes remain, but most have been remodeled beyond recognition or replaced by more substantial residences.

The docks themselves are private property, and you will see signage to that effect. Should you still decide to take a stroll along one in spite of the warnings, please remember that these are people's homes – peering into windows, taking photographs, and general rambunctiousness are frowned upon. My wife, Jennifer, who lived on one of these houseboats during her college days, says that most people don't notice the occasional tourist, but a friend who both lives and *works* on his houseboat, insists that tourists drive his neighbors crazy (he suggests rolling a ball along the dock, and if questioned, say you're just retrieving the errant plaything). In all honesty, we've never been confronted by residents, but just in case, we chose docks with "For Sale" signs at the end, providing the convenient excuse that we are "shopping."

If you continue north on Fairview to E Roanoke, you will come to a second community of larger, newer houseboats.

Downtown

National Oceanographic and Atmospheric Administration (NOAA)

1801 Fairview Ave. E
(206) 553-4548

The vessels docked here are NOAA survey ships whose mission is to map the ocean floor, monitor the weather and environment, and other marine science-related endeavors. If you are interested in a guided tour, they can be scheduled on weekdays during the winter. Phone to make arrangements.

Incidentally, if your teenager is still unsure about what to do after graduation, I've known several people who signed on for hitches with NOAA and swear by it – a real public service adventure that does not involve learning to shoot guns at people.

Float Plane Air Tours

South end of Lake Union
Cost: Varies

If you want to give your family an experience they will never forget, a flight on a float plane can't be beat. Both of the operators listed here offer relatively inexpensive (approximately $60 per person), 20-minute air tours of Seattle. You can also take longer air tours that include the San Juan Islands and Mt. Rainier, although you can pretty much charter any kind of trip your family desires. Ask about packages that include lunch and ground transportation at your destination.

My wife, Jennifer, once surprised me with a flight to Port Ludlow for a birthday dinner at the resort. My brother arranged the same thing for his groomsmen before his wedding.

Keep in mind that people with a fear of heights, water, or a tendency toward claustrophobia might find these tiny planes too much to take.

National Oceanographic and Atmospheric Administration (NOAA)

Directions: (See directions to Lake Union.) From Fairview Ave. N, turn right onto Eastlake Ave., then continue to E Blaine St. and turn left. NOAA is on Fairview Ave. E at the foot of Blaine. On-street parking.

Kenmore Air

950 Westlake Ave. N

(206) 369-6990

Directions: (See directions to Lake Union.) From Fairview Ave. N, turn left onto Westlake Ave. N, get immediately into the right lane, then look for the parking lot, which is just beyond the Center for Wooden Boats.

Seattle Seaplanes

1325 Fairview Ave. E

(206) 329-9638

www.seattleseaplanes.com

Directions: (See directions to Lake Union.) From Fairview Ave. N, turn right onto Eastlake Ave. Bear left onto Fairview Ave. E. Parking lot entrance will be on your left.

Downtown

"Duck Dodge" sailboat races

Lake Union

On Tuesday evenings from late spring through early fall, all manner of sailing vessels take to the waters of Lake Union for the informal and highly goofy "Duck Dodge" race.

Rent a boat at the Center for Wooden Boats (see above) and join in, or just watch from the marina at the south end of the lake.

Gasworks Park is another good viewing venue (see North Seattle chapter).

Safe N' Sound Swimming

2040 Westlake Ave. N
(206) 285-9279

Safe N' Sound Swimming

Cost: $13 per lesson, plus $25 registration fee.

Hours: Mon.-Sat., 9 a.m. - 7 p.m.

Directions: (See directions to Lake Union.) From Fairview Ave. N, turn left onto Westlake Ave. N, get immediately into the right lane and follow Westlake around to the west side of Lake Union. Continue for about a mile. Turn right into free parking lot. SNS is under the giant, black China Harbor restaurant. Go down the stairs on the south side of the building.

If you have time for a session of swimming lessons, there is no better place in Seattle than this indoor pool. The teachers are generally a cut above the temporary crews that run the city's programs and some are brilliant. These are 15-minute one-on-one lessons. I avoided coming here for years, thinking that the short lessons wouldn't be worth the effort, until I did the simple math (i.e., an hour long class with four children, leaves my child with the same 15 minutes of instruction). Josephine is exhausted and hungry after these intensive sessions. As she so succinctly puts it: "It was hard, but it was fun!" After only a few months of weekly lessons, she was swimming.

Downtown

Places to Eat

Cucina! Cucina!

901 Fairview Ave. N.
(206) 447-2782

Cucina! Cucina!

Directions: (See directions to Lake Union.) From Fairview Ave. N, turn right, then immediately left into the free parking lot.

Of all the restaurants crammed onto the southern shore of Lake Union, this is the best non-fast food option for taking a hungry family. The Italian fare is pretty good and should offer something for even picky eaters. The restaurant was intentionally designed to be noisy – even when the place is relatively empty, the kitchen clatter alone causes voices to rise. During the lunch and dinner rush, even a shrieking child will barely turn a head.

Daly's

Eastlake Ave. E
(206) 322-1918

Daly's

Directions: (See directions to Lake Union.) From Fairview Ave. N, turn right onto Eastlake Ave. and continue to the corner of Roanoke St. Free parking lot.

When I first met my wife-to-be, Jennifer, nearly 20 years ago, she introduced me to this funky fast food venue, and I've been hooked ever since. I've always had the steak sandwich (with extra sauce) and onion rings, although friends swear by the burgers and fries as well. Sit at the counter by the window for peek-a-boo views of Lake Union, the Space Needle, and the rest of Seattle's skyline.

There are three vintage 25¢ pinball machines and a couple of nostalgia inducing video games (*Ms. Pac Man* for one) to occupy your time as you await your cooked-to-order meal.

It had been awhile since I'd eaten here, so in the interest of preparing this book, I returned and nothing, from menu to décor, has changed. Special sauce is automatically applied to everything, so if you or your child don't like mayonnaise-based product on your sandwich, say so in advance.

2 North Seattle

For the sake of this book, "North Seattle" refers to everything north of the Lake Washington Ship Canal, although I've (quite arbitrarily) included Magnolia and Queen Anne in this section.

Before Josephine was born, we lived in View Ridge, a quiet, tidy neighborhood of middle class homes, which is more or less indicative of the majority of Seattle's north end. There are pockets of wealth and poverty, but for the most part you will find modest homes, decent schools, family-oriented restaurants, and lots of European faces. That said, each neighborhood has its own personality, influenced by its history (such as Ballard), natural features (such as Green Lake), or institutions (such as the University District). Although we currently live in South Seattle, Josephine's school is in the north and most of her friends live in these neighborhoods, drawing us northward on an almost daily basis.

If you have the chance, walk around these neighborhoods. There are many more family activities than those we've been able to include in this book.

A Parent's Guide to Seattle

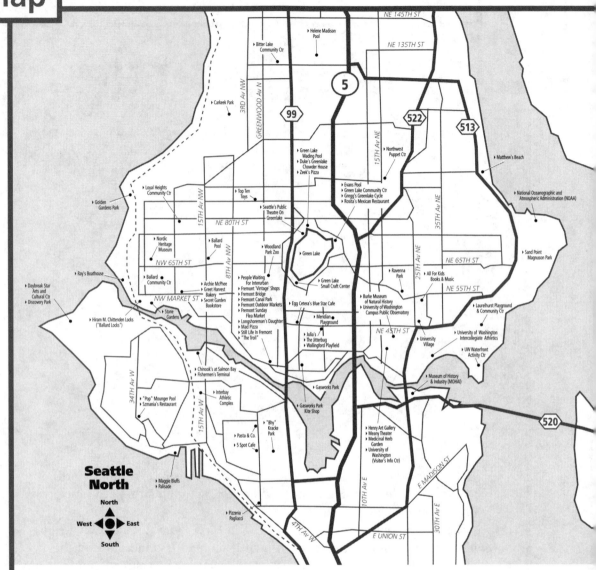

NE 145TH ST

NE 135TH ST

Helene Madison Pool

Bitter Lake Community Ctr

5

99

522

513

3RD AV NW

GREENWOOD AV N

Carkeek Park

Green Lake Wading Pool
Duke's Greenlake Chowder House
Zeek's Pizza

15TH AV NE

Northwest Puppet Ctr

Matthew's Beach

Evans Pool
Green Lake Community Ctr
Gregg's Greenlake Cycle
Rosita's Mexican Restaurant

National Oceanographic and Atmospheric Administration (NOAA)

Loyal Heights Community Ctr

Golden Gardens Park

Top Ten Toys

Seattle's Public Theatre On Greenlake

15TH AV NW

NE 80TH ST

8TH AV NW

35TH AV NE

Nordic Heritage Museum

Ballard Pool

Woodland Park Zoo

Green Lake

Sand Point Magnuson Park

NW 65TH ST

Ray's Boathouse

Ballard Community Ctr

Archie McPhee
Greet Harvest Bakery
Secret Garden Bookstore

People Waiting For Interurban
Fremont 'Vintage' Shops
Fremont Bridge
Fremont Canal Park
Fremont Outdoor Markets
Fremont Sunday Flea Market
Longshoreman's Daughter
Mad Pizza
Still Life In Fremont
"The Troll"

Green Lake Small Craft Center

Ravenna Park

All For Kids Books & Music

NE 65TH ST

Daybreak Star Arts and Cultural Ctr
Discovery Park

Hiram M. Chittenden Locks ("Ballard Locks")

Store Gardens

NW MARKET ST

Burke Museum of Natural History
University of Washington Campus Public Observatory

NE 55TH ST

25TH AV NE

Laurelhurst Playground & Community Ctr

Egg Cetera's Blue Star Cafe

Meridian Playground

Julia's
The Jitterbug
Wallingford Playfield

NE 45TH ST

University Village

University of Washington Intercollegiate Athletics

UW Waterfront Activity Ctr

34TH AV W

Chinook's at Salmon Bay
Fishermen's Terminal

Gasworks Park

Museum of History & Industry (MOHAI)

520

"Pop" Mounger Pool
Szmania's Restaurant

Interbay Athletic Complex

15TH AV W

Gasworks Park Kite Shop

"Bhy" Kracke Park

Henry Art Gallery
Meany Theater
Medicinal Herb Garden
University of Washington (Visitor's Info Ctr)

10TH AV E

E MADISON ST

Pasta & Co.

5 Spot Cafe

Seattle North

North

West ◀◆▶ East

South

Maggie Bluffs
Palisade

30TH AV E

Pizzeria Pagliacci

4TH AV W

E UNION ST

North Seattle

Ballard

**Ballard is bordered by 3rd Ave NW on the east,
Shilshole Bay on the west,
the ship canal/Salmon Bay to the south,
and NW 85th St. to the north.**

Ballard

Directions: From I-5 north or south, take the 45th St. exit (#169) and head west. Continue west. After a couple of miles the street name will change to N Market St., then NW Market St. Once you've crossed 3rd Ave NW you are in Ballard, but continue about a mile-and-a-half to Leary Way and you will be in the heart of Ballard. On-street parking.

Long the punch line to Seattle jokes about its reputation as insular and provincial, Ballard has become one of the city's top neighborhoods for young families and visitors alike. Ballard's Scandinavian identity has more to do with its history as an immigrant neighborhood and its community events and retailers, than its current population, which is increasingly multi-ethnic.

Still, the annual Norwegian Constitution Day Parade, May 17, is among the five largest in the world, and the Nordic Heritage Museum (see below) is widely acknowledged as one of the top heritage museums anywhere. The Ballard Merchants Nordic Holidays Celebration (which begins Thanksgiving weekend) is always a popular way to kick-off the holiday season.

courtesy Army Corps of Engineers

Ballard Locks and Canal

North Seattle

Things to Do

Hiram M. Chittenden Locks ("Ballard Locks")

3015 NW 54th St.
(206) 783-7059 (visitor center)
www.nws.usace.army.mil/opdiv/lwsc

courtesy Army Corps of Engineers

Ships use the canal

If you only have time for one off-the-beaten-path destination while visiting the Seattle area, I would recommend that you visit what locals refer to as the "Ballard Locks." This project by the Army Corps of Engineers is a combination of features: two navigational locks, a dam and spillway, a fish ladder, a botanical garden, and a regional visitor center and bookstore.

The Visitor Center is a good first stop. Here you will find displays on the history and operation of the canal and locks. This is also where free guided tours begin, provided daily during the summer and on weekends the rest of the year.

The English-style garden is beautiful in the spring and summer with its 500+ species of plant life, but frankly, the lure of the locks and fish ladder tend to prevent us from spending a whole lot of time here.

The dam, locks, and fish ladder are where it's at. The gates of the dam release or store water required to maintain the lake at about 20-22 feet above sea level. The elevation is necessary for the floating bridges, mooring facilities, and vessel clearance under bridges. The locks act as a kind of marine elevator for boats passing between the lower salt water of Salmon Bay and the higher fresh water of Lake Union. It's a fun process to watch as the gates (complete with flashing lights and warning bells) open to allow boats of all sizes into the chamber. When the gates close, observers can venture out atop them to witness the filling or draining of the chamber. When the water pressure is equal on both sides, the gates are opened again.

Cross the locks and the dam to the opposite side of the canal to the fish ladder. When the locks and dam were built in 1916, they blocked all the salmon runs of the Cedar River watershed. The fish ladder allows salmon to pass around the locks and dam on their way to and from their spawning grounds. You can watch from the outside (where

Hiram M. Chittenden Locks

Cost: Free

Directions: Continue west on NW Market St. to NW 54th St. Turn left into the free parking lot.

North Seattle

Josephine and I once saw scientists capturing, tagging, and releasing adult salmon) or, better, from the indoor public viewing gallery where you are only inches away from the migrating fish. July, August, and September are the best months for viewing fish in the ladder when the sockeye, coho, and king salmon have their runs, although there can be fish in the ladder year-round (the peak of the steelhead run is in February and March).

The parks on either side of the canal are great for play and picnics. The grounds are frequently used during the summer for outdoor concerts and other events. Call for a schedule.

Restrooms are usually clean. Even during spring and fall, it can be windy, so come prepared.

courtesy Army Corps of Engineers

courtesy Army Corps of Engineers

And there's a great view!

North Seattle

Nordic Heritage Museum

3014 NW 67th St.
(206) 789-5707
www.nordicmuseum.com

Okay, so this might not sound like a place your children will *want* to visit, but they will be pleasantly surprised, especially if you plan your visit to coincide with the "Tivoli" celebration (typically in June), the "Yule Fest" (mid-November), or one of the

Kids in traditional Norwegian costumes

courtesy Nordic Heritage Museum

dozens of special children's activities throughout the year. Check the website or phone for a calendar of these popular events, most of which require reservations.

The focus of the 50,000 square foot, 3-storey museum is on the experiences of immigrants from Sweden, Denmark, Norway, Finland, and Iceland; their costumes, art, and culture.

Nordic Heritage Museum

Cost: Adults $4, seniors/college students $3, children (K-12) $2, under K free.

Hours: Tues.-Sat., 10 a.m. - 4 p.m.; Sun., 12 p.m. - 4 p.m.

Directions: From NW Market St., head north on 28th Ave. NW to NW 67th St. Turn left and the museum will be on your right.

Fishermen's Terminal

3919 18th Ave. W

Across the Ballard Bridge, Fishermen's Terminal is the homeport of the Alaskan fishing fleet. It's fun to stroll up and down the docks for an up-close look at

Fishermen's Terminal

Directions: From NW Market St., head south on 15th Ave. NW, cross the Ballard Bridge and follow the signs to Fisherman's Terminal.

these working vessels. The Fishermen's Memorial is a bronze and stone sculpture erected to honor the 500+ local commercial fishermen and women who have been lost at sea since the beginning of the 20th century. Each year on the first Sunday of May, a very moving service is held to honor all those who have died pursuing their livelihood and, sadly, to place additional names on the plaques.

There are a few retail businesses here, and Chinook's restaurant (see below) is a great place for a family meal. Public restrooms.

North Seattle

Golden Gardens Park

8499 Seaview Pl. NW
www.cityofseattle.net/parks

A fantastic summertime sandy beach, albeit without lifeguards. Children love playing in the shallow (ankle deep) creek that flows into Shilshole Bay; damming it up to create their own wading pools, redirecting the flow with sand and rocks, or following it under the pedestrian bridge to its "source." Beach fires are allowed, which means the sand is generously mixed with ash – but you'll have to take baths afterward anyway.

> **Golden Gardens Park**
>
> Directions: Take NW Market St. W, bear left onto NW 54th, passing the Hiram Chittenden Locks. The street name then changes to Seaview. Follow Seaview as it turns northward all the way to the park. Ample free parking in the lots.

During cooler months, we like to take a walk northward along the beach and explore the wetlands area, where ducks, turtles, and other wildlife abound. I especially recommend Golden Gardens during extreme low tides, when the tidal habitat is exposed for a few hours at a time – starfish, anemones, crabs, jellyfish, and other creatures are plentiful. Bring rubber boots, and please don't remove anything from the beach.

On clear days, the views of the Olympic Mountains are spectacular. All play stops as children watch the frequent trains that pass through the park on an elevated track.

There is a very basic playground with surprisingly clean restrooms.

Ballard Community Center

6020 28th Ave. NW
(206) 684-4093
www.ci.seattle.wa.us/parks/Centers/Ballard.htm

The Ballard Community Center offers a wide array of programs and special events for children and their families, including after school care, tot programs, an extensive dance program, piano, pottery, t-ball, day camps, and dozens of other offerings. Special events occur throughout the year and include an annual daddy-daughter dinner, spring egg hunt, a neighborhood flea market, and family dance nights. Call for schedule.

> **Ballard Community Center**
>
> Cost: Call for program fees.
>
> Hours:
> Mon.-Fri., 9 a.m. - 9 p.m.;
> Sat., 9 a.m. - 5 p.m.
> Closed Sun. and city holidays.
>
> Directions: From NW Market St., head north on 28th Ave NW. The community center is on the right just after you cross NW 60th.

North Seattle

The playground features a large boat half-buried in sand for climbing.

The community center is also one of 10 offering the Kidsplace program which provides low-income families with quality, positive education and fun activities for school-age children in an inclusive, safe, and nurturing environment in order to meet after school child care needs of Seattle's families. Activities include homework/tutoring; arts and crafts; games, sports, and other recreational opportunities. Call for information.

Ballard Pool

1471 NW 67th St.
(206) 684-4094
www.ci.seattle.wa.us/parks/Aquatics/Ballardp.htm

This is a fun, indoor community pool, kept somewhat warmer than some of the other city pools. There is a 1-meter diving board, rope swing and slide (extra fee, except during special open swim times). Our friend Tevan (6-years-old) loves the warm water pool, kept between 98-102 degrees, which is too hot for Josephine. There are 2 family changing rooms. Children must meet the minimum height requirement of 4 feet tall or be accompanied in the pool by an adult on a one-to-one ratio.

Ballard Pool

Cost: Adult $2.50; youth (1-18) $1.75; under 1 are free (call for additional fees for programs).

Hours: Varies by season. Call ahead. Closed for Labor Day, Veteran's Day, Thanksgiving (2 days), Christmas, New Year's Day, Martin Luther King Day, and President's Day.

Directions: From NW Market St., head north on 15th Ave. NW. Turn right onto NW 67th St. The pool will be on your right.

Loyal Heights Community Center

2101 NW 77th St.
(206) 684-4052
www.ci.seattle.wa.us/parks/Centers/Loyalhtd.htm

The Loyal Heights Community Center offers classes and special events for families such as after school care, toddler programs, gymnastics, piano, karate, t-ball, day camps, and dozens of other offerings. Special events throughout the year include an annual pancake breakfast, a spring egg hunt, and chess tournaments. Loyal Heights features an extensive early childhood education program which includes a pre-school as well as Play Center classes which focus on building social, physical, and educational skills. Call for details.

The facility has recently added a weight room for adult use.

Loyal Heights Community Center

Cost: Call for program costs.

Hours: Mon.-Fri., 9 a.m. - 9 p.m.; Sat.-Sun., 9 a.m. - 5 p.m. Closed for all city holidays.

Directions: From NW Market St., head north on 22nd NW. The community center is on the corner of 22nd and NW 77th.

North Seattle

Stone Gardens

2839 NW Market Street
(206) 781-9828
www.stonegardens.com

This magnificent indoor facility features some 14,000 square feet of "rock" climbing walls for all ability levels, but will be too challenging for most children under 5.

If your children have experience, they can climb on their own; if not, you might want to try the "Kids Climb" classes, with a ratio of one instructor for every 4 students. Classes for older and more experienced climbers are also available. Registration is required, so call first.

Equipment can be rented. The facility is available for parties as is the "portable" climbing wall, which can be brought to you!

Weeklong summer camp programs are offered for children as young as 5. With a 2:1 student-teacher ratio, even the youngest children should be safe.

Parents must sign a waiver for all children under 18.

Stone Gardens

Day rates: Adults $12; children (17 and under) $10.

Hours: Mon., Wed., Fri. & Sat., 10 a.m. - 10 p.m.;
Tues. & Thurs., 6 a.m. - 11 p.m.;
Sun., 10 a.m. - 7 p.m.

Directions: From I-5 take the 45th St. exit (#169) and head west on 45th until it turns into NW Market St. Continue on Market through Ballard. Stone Gardens is located on the left across from Taco Time.

North Seattle

Places to Eat

Chinook's at Salmon Bay

1900 W Nickerson St.
(206) 283-4665

Located at Fishermen's Terminal, Chinook's is a large, family-friendly restaurant with nice views of Salmon Bay and boats moored in the marina. Seafood is the specialty.

Chinook's at Salmon Bay

Directions: See directions to Fisherman's Terminal (above).

Hours: Mon.-Thurs., 11 a.m. - 10 p.m., Fri. 11 a.m. - 11 p.m., Sat. 7:30 a.m. - 11 p.m., Sun. 7:30 a.m. - 10 p.m.

Great Harvest Bakery

2218 NW Market St.
(206) 706-3434
greatharvest.uswestdex.com

Great bakery, great people. Fantastic seasonal baked goods – we bought an Easter bunny loaf for a centerpiece, ate it on the bus ride home, and had to go back for another.

Ray's Boathouse

6049 Seaview Ave. NW
(206) 789-3770
www.rays.com/boathouse.html

Ray's Boathouse is a Seattle's seafood icon. The food is simply and elegantly prepared, and the views of Puget Sound and the Olympic Mountains – particularly at sunset – are unsurpassed. All other seafood restaurants aspire to be like Ray's.

It's not cheap, nor does it cater to young children. I include this because if you were my guest, and you wanted to have one nice dinner in Seattle, this is the place I would take you.

Ray's Boathouse

Hours: Mon.-Thurs., 5 p.m. - 9 p.m.; Fri., 5 p.m. - 10 p.m.; Sat., 4:30 p.m. - 10 p.m.; Sun., 4:30 p.m. - 9 p.m.

Directions: Continue west on NW Market St. until it intersects with Seaview Ave. NW. Turn right. Ray's will be on your left.

North Seattle

Places to Shop

Archie McPhee

2428 NW Market St.
(206) 297-0240
www.mcphee.com

I don't like to aimlessly shop, and particularly not with Josephine ("Will you buy me this? Will you buy me that? Why not? Why not? Will you buy me this?"), but I'll come here any day of the week alone or with daughter in tow.

You'll know you're here by the giant frilled lizard head above the door and human hand chairs on the sidewalk. It's the dimestore toy aisle of your youth on steroids, and they still have dozens of items that cost a dime (or even a nickel) and hundreds of things under $1. Need size 74 underpants or a green beehive hairdo wig? This is the place. Backward clock? Giant feet? Rabbi punching puppets? Portable urinal? Novelties, candies, charms, and an odd assortment of medical supplies fill the shelves of this mecca of kitsch, nostalgia, and fun. A great place to put together Halloween costumes.

The staff is young, friendly, and obviously customers of the store.

On dull, rainy days, I give Josephine a dollar and we idle away an hour (or more) trying to spend it here. Not only does she have fun choosing her "loot," but we also gain experience in money management.

courtesy Archie McPhee

Archie McPhee store front

North Seattle

Secret Garden Bookstore
2214 NW Market St.
(206) 789-5006

There are bigger bookstores and there are cheaper bookstores, but there are no *better* bookstores for children than the Secret Garden. It's the staff that makes it so good – they've actually read the books and have the knowledge and insight to help you choose the right book for your child. One of the best uses of their knowledge is when you need a book to help your child with a specific problem or issue. For instance: "My 6-year-old is hung up on getting presents instead of appreciating the true meaning of the holidays," or "My 8-year-old is having trouble with a bully." They'll have recommendations that are both subject and age appropriate. Call for reading times.

Fremont

Fremont's boundaries are the canal on the south,
8th Ave. NW on the west, North 50th Street on the north,
and Stone Way on the east.

Fremont

Directions: From I-5 north or south, take the 45th St. exit and head east on 45th. After about a mile, turn left on Stone Way. Follow Stone Way to N 34th St. and turn right. Turn right onto Fremont Ave. N and you will be in the heart of Fremont. Limited street parking and pay lots.

The self-proclaimed "center of the universe," Fremont is indeed the center of all that is wacky, wild, and oddball about Seattle. This is where a walk around the neighborhood will reveal a second-hand shop under the shadow of a giant silver rocket ship, a cold-war era statue of Vladimir Lenin, a troll hiding under a bridge, a neon Rapunzel locked in a tower, a bus stop full of cast-aluminum commuters with an ever-changing wardrobe, a topiary dinosaur, and an endless parade of hippies, techies, and yuppies.

Fremont, nestled on the shores of the Lake Washington Ship Canal is home to dozens of funky, kitschy shops, antique and "vintage" stores, and some good restaurants. It's a place to park the car and explore.

North Seattle

Things to Do

The Troll

**Under the north end of the Aurora Bridge on
N 36th St. between Wallingford and Fremont.**

courtesy Army Corps of Engineers

The Troll

This might be Seattle's favorite piece of public art – an enormous, creepy concrete troll with a ski-slope nose, who appears to be munching on a vintage Volkswagen Beetle (created by a team of local artists). Kids love to climb on it, but you will want to police the area first for broken glass and other garbage. It's not a Disney character, and Josephine was frightened by it when she was younger, but now insists that we at least do a drive-by whenever we're in the neighborhood. We joke that the troll's job is to eat illegally parked cars, which is a common sight in this parking-challenged area.

People Waiting for Interurban

Fremont Ave. N and N 34th St.

Ranking alongside the troll in the hearts of "Fremonsters," *People Waiting for Interurban* (Richard Beyer, 1978) features a small knot of cast-aluminum commuters waiting under a pergola for their bus. The sculpture's grimness is apparently seen as a challenge to the color-loving locals who dress and decorate the piece to celebrate birthdays, anniversaries, or just for fun. In my 15 years in Seattle, I've never seen the statue "naked." See how long it takes your children to figure out what's wrong with the dog (dog's body; human face).

Fremont Bridge

Fremont Ave. N and N 34th St.

Known to Josephine as the "orange bridge" (actually orange and blue), this drawbridge over the Lake Washington Ship Canal was for a long time Fremont's primary connection to its "suburb" with the tall towers. Take a walk across it and spot the neon Rapunzel locked in the tower. Children love to sit in the parks along either shore of the canal and watch the bridge rise to let tall ships through.

North Seattle

Fremont Canal Park

N 34th St., two blocks west of Fremont Ave. N

This greenway park along the shore of the Lake Washington Ship Canal is a nice place for a picnic, views of shipping traffic, and a great vantage point from which to watch the drawbridge operate (there is a shelter at the west end of the park which gives the best view). Topiary dinosaurs stand guard at the entrance from N 34th. Watch your little ones, as there is nothing to prevent them from tumbling into the water. The "sidewalk" here is part of the Burke-Gilman trail and, as such, is used by cyclists, some of whom don't slow down for small children.

Fremont Sunday Flea Market

3416 Evanston Ave. N (inside the Adobe Building)
(206) 282-5706

If this market were staged anywhere else, it would just be another collection of craft booths and junk, but in Fremont it becomes a community celebration. You'll find something you want to buy and you'll likely find it cheap.

Fremont Outdoor Movies

N 34th St. and Phinney Ave. N
(206) 781-4230
www.outdoorfilmfestival.com

During summer months, these outdoor screenings of movies that range from popular comedies to classics to bizarre B-movies are events unto themselves, drawing both families and (gentle) freaks of all description. Your children will love the fact that cheering, talking, and shouting at the screen is not only tolerated, but encouraged. The fun often includes live entertainment, contests, and vendors.

The venue is a parking lot, so bring your own seating. Also, you should call first – there may be some movies that you don't want your children to see.

North Seattle

Places to Eat

Mad Pizza

3601 Fremont Ave. N, Ste. 101
(206) 632-5453

This outpost of the local chain can quickly get a decent slice into you and yours. They have no problem with noisy, messy kids (maybe because they are noisy, messy kids themselves).

Still Life in Fremont

705 N 35th St.
(206) 547-9850

This 1960s throwback coffee house might just be the center of the "center of the universe." Usually, we are here for the yummy baked goods, but the soups and sandwiches are also outstanding. Seating can be tough right at lunchtime.

Simply Desserts

3421 Fremont Ave. N
(206) 633-2671

This is one of the best dessert places in Seattle. Cakes, torts, cookies . . . everything is good.

Longshoreman's Daughter

3508 Fremont Place N
(206) 633-5169

Cheap, hip, diner-café fare. Breakfast is an emphasis, but you'll probably have to wait. Local and national celebrities are often spotted here. A Fremont institution.

Mad Pizza
Hours:
11 a.m. - 10 p.m., Daily

Still Life in Fremont
Hours:
7:30 a.m. - 9 p.m., Daily

Simply Desserts
Hours:
Tues.-Thurs. 12 p.m. - 10 p.m.
Fri.-Sat. 12 p.m. - 11:30 p.m.
Sun. 12 p.m. - 6 p.m.

Longshoreman's Daughter
Hours:
Mon.-Fri., 7:30 a.m. - 10 p.m.;
Sat.-Sun., 7:30 a.m. - 2:30 p.m.;
Sat.-Sun., 3:30 p.m. - 10 p.m.

North Seattle

Places to Shop

"Vintage" shops

Fremont is home to a plethora of shops specializing in all manner of "vintage" and antique home furnishings, art, decoration, clothing, toys, and just about anything else you can imagine. Wander around – even your children should have fun doing this.

Gasworks Park Kite Shop

3420 Stone Way N
(206) 633-4780

Yes, you can buy a kite here – for as little as $6 or as much as $350 – but that's just where it begins. This is essentially a "fun in the park" shop, including bubbles, yo-yos, sidewalk chalk, and all manner of throwing and flying toys. The staff is friendly and knows more than people ought to about flying kites.

Green Lake

E Green Lake Dr. N and W Green Lake Dr. N

One of the most popular recreational areas in the city (more than 1 million visitors per year), Green Lake attracts skaters, cyclists, walkers, joggers, basketball players, swimmers, and athletes of nearly every description, age, and talent level. The primary lure is the nearly 3-mile paved path that encircles the lake. The path is divided in half, one side for "feet," the other for "wheels" (strollers count as "feet"). Don't expect everyone to strictly adhere to these distinctions. You will need to watch out for the occasional speed demons on wheels or – by the same token – pedestrians who blithely meander over the line into "traffic." When strolling with toddlers, I find that both they and I enjoy ourselves more by staying on the grass, exploring amongst the trees (many of which are identified by species by small signs on their trunks) or down by the water's edge.

Green Lake

Directions: From I-5 (north or south), take exit #169, 45th/50th Street exits. Choose the 50th Street lane, turn left at the light, proceed west along 50th Street to a five-way stop light, where Stone Way N turns into Green Lake Way N, and turn right onto Green Lake Way North (Lower Woodland Park's ball fields will then be on your left). Get in the left lane and continue for about eight city blocks. Take the left turn lane (a mini-golf course is in front of you – go left so the golf course is on your right) onto West Green Lake Way N. The parking lot on the northeast side of the park is inadequate for demand during the summer and on sunny days. The lot on the northwest side is better, but you might find yourself hunting for un-metered street parking.

North Seattle

Green Lake

The northeast side of the park is home to the indoor Evans Pool and Community Center (see below). You will also find public tennis courts, a swimming beach (with lifeguards during summer months), canoe and paddleboat rentals (see below), sports fields, and a large, new, well-equipped playground.

A wildly popular wading pool is located at the north end of the park (see below).

The Bathhouse Theater (see below) is on the northwest side of the park as is a second swimming beach with summer-time lifeguards.

The southern part of the park features the Green Lake Small Craft Center (see below), a pitch and putt golf course (the putting green is fun for small children), as well as lawn bowling and horseshoe courts.

Things to Do

Evans Pool

Northeast side of Green Lake in the community center
(206) 684-4961
www.ci.seattle.wa.us/seattle/aquatics

Evans Pool

Recreation program fees: Adults $2.50, children $1.75 (various multi-use passes available).

Hours: Call for specific program times. Closed Thanksgiving, Christmas, Labor Day, Veteran's Day, New Year's Day.

We aren't the only ones who complain that they keep the water in this indoor swimming pool too cold for children, but they do it because it's more comfortable for the lap swimmers who comprise the largest segment of the pool's users. Children under 4 feet tall and/or 6 years of age must be accompanied in the water by an adult. Swimming lessons are available as are pool rentals for such things as birthday parties. Call for times and fees. A family changing room in available.

Evans Pool

North Seattle

Green Lake Community Center

Northeast side of Green Lake
(206) 684-0780

In addition to housing Evans Pool (see above), the community center features both indoor and outdoor basketball courts, pool, ping-pong and foosball tables, a weight room, and a wide assortment of adult and children's classes and sports programs, ranging from art, dance, and chess to martial arts, yoga, and flag football. The toddler play center is a fun rainy day activity for children 5 and under. There are many toys for children including climbing frames, see-saws, learn to walk bikes, play houses, blocks, cars, trucks, dolls, and buggies. The Seattle Homeschool Group also meets here on a regular basis to work on projects. The group is open to all and is free. Call (206) 789-1069 for information.

> **Green Lake Community Center**
>
> Fees: Vary depending on program.
>
> Toddler Play Center: $1 per child; $35 annual pass.
>
> Hours: Mon.-Fri., 10 a.m. - 10 p.m.;
> Sat., 10 a.m. - 5 p.m.; Sun., 12 p.m. - 4 p.m.
> Closed Thanksgiving and Christmas days.
>
> Play Center hours: Mon.-Fri., 10 a.m. - 9 p.m.;
> Sat., 10 a.m. - 4 p.m.; Sun., 12 p.m. - 3:30 p.m.

Green Lake Boat Rental

5900 W Green Lake Way N (in the park, along the northeast side of the lake)
(206) 527-0171

Older children (14+) who can swim and have some experience handling a small boat can rent their own canoe, kayak, wind surfboard, sailboat, or paddle boat for a few turns around the lake on their own. An adult with swimming skills should accompany younger children. Life jackets are provided, but they won't fit very small children properly. If your child is under 30 lbs., bring your own infant/toddler life jacket. You needn't worry about being terrorized by motorized boats, as they are not allowed on Green Lake.

courtesy Seattle Parks/Recreation

North Seattle

Seattle's Public Theater on Green Lake ("Bathhouse Theater")

7312 W Green Lake Dr. N
(206) 325-6500 (tickets)
(206) 328-4848 (youth program information and administration)
www.seattlepublictheater.org

Seattle's Public Theater on Green Lake
Cost: Call for ticket prices and show times.
Directions: Traveling north on I-5, take 65th St./Ravenna exit. Turn left on 65th St. Bear right onto Ravenna Blvd. for .3 miles. Bear right onto E Greenlake Dr. N. Continue past the stoplight until you can turn left into a parking lot. The theater is located only a short walk towards the lake.
Traveling south on I-5, take the NE 70th St. exit. Turn right on NE 70th St. Turn right on E Green Lake Dr. N. Continue past the stoplight until you can turn left into a parking lot. The theater is located only a short walk towards the lake.

Located in the historic brick Green Lake Bathhouse, most locals refer to this as the "Bathhouse Theater." You will want to call first for details, but children's theater performances are generally held on Saturday afternoons and kiddie shows Saturday and Wednesday mornings. After school classes and programs are offered throughout the year for children K-12.

Green Lake Wading Pool

N 73rd St. & W Green Lake Way
(206) 684-7796 (aquatic info. hotline)

The pool is filled each morning during the summer months, chlorinated, and emptied each evening (as with all City of Seattle wading pools). I know it doesn't sound so great, but Josephine loves for us to show up when the pool is empty (usually around 11 a.m., although it varies according to the weather and whims of staffers) and stand along the side as it is filled. I mention this because she is apparently not alone. There are always dozens of kids standing around waiting for the parks and rec staffer (not a lifeguard!) to give them the go-ahead. My only complaint (and this is also true of all City of Seattle wading pools) is that there are times when the pool is overwhelmed by rowdy gangs of day-campers being overseen by a handful of supervisors who are little more than teenagers themselves. Older children don't mind – in fact they tend to join in the ruckus – but younger children can be intimidated.

North Seattle

Green Lake Small Craft Center

7201 East Green Lake Drive N
(206) 684-4074
www.ci.seattle.wa.us/parks/boats/grnlake.htm

Green Lake from above

Located at the southwest corner of the lake, the center offers adult and youth classes in rowing, canoeing, kayaking, and sailing. Participants must be at least 13-years-old and pass a "float test." Call for details.

The center hosts three major rowing regattas during the year, the largest being the Frostbite Regatta in November, which draws competitors from throughout the Northwest. Other regattas are held during the spring and summer. You might not want to spend an entire day as a spectator, but an hour or two can be both entertaining and perhaps even inspirational.

Woodland Park Zoo

5500 Phinney Ave. N
(206) 684-4800
www.zoo.org

Widely recognized as one of the top zoos in the U.S., Woodland Park Zoo is a place we've visited dozens of times since Josephine was born. In fact, during the spring and summer, we've been known to visit weekly.

You'll find the usual assortment of exotic wild animals – lions, gorillas, tigers, zebras, giraffes, elephants, hippos – all living in "habitats" rather than pacing in cages. (You will find one empty cage left intact as a reminder of how things used to be.) It's fun to see the herbivores (giraffes, zebras, hippos, etc.) living together, for instance, on the "African Savanna," rather than artificially separated as they were in the zoos of my youth.

The 6-acre exhibit of animals found in the Northwest (the Northern Trail) is thrilling, especially when the bears are frolicking in the water only inches from where your youngsters' faces are pressed to the glass. The playful otters are a hit as well – when they're up to their antics, it's impossible to drag yourself away, not to mention your kids. Wolves, elk, shaggy mountain goats, and other Northwest animals also call this exhibit home.

North Seattle

The elephant house is another special place (bath time at 10 a.m.; call for a schedule of "elephant shows") as is the expansive indoor-outdoor orangutan exhibit. If Josephine only had a playground like this one, she tells me, she would never ask for anything else.

Designed with younger children in mind, the Family Farm area is home to a wide variety of domestic farm animals, many of which (such as bunnies, goats, and sheep) are available for petting and feeding during the spring, summer, and early fall. I've never visited the adjacent Bug World house with my child due to her squeamishness around all things "creepy-crawly," but our insect-ophilic friends give it raves.

Josephine's favorite zoo activity is watching the penguins' 11 a.m. feeding time, then taking a pony ride ($2 at our last visit – warmer months only).

If your kids have had it with animals, the Habitat Discovery Loop playground is a one-of-a-kind adventure featuring a giant "spider web" for climbing, a maze of "burrows" for spelunking, "rock" slides, and other zoo and habitat-related apparatuses.

The zoo staff is friendly, knowledgeable, and eager to answer questions – often stepping in to settle debates unsolicited. One incredibly patient woman in the raptor arena spent 15 minutes answering the highly repetitive questions of then 3-year-old Josephine and her friend Elly. Years later, Josephine still remembers learning that the bald eagle (which was raised in captivity) thinks it's human.

I highly recommend bringing your own picnic lunch to the zoo. Food is available, but it is largely of the junk, junk, and more junk variety.

Sunny days and summer weekends bring in the crowds, so if you can manage it, choose a weekday or take advantage of overcast days to cover more ground in less time.

Strollers are available for rent, but they are not allowed in all areas of the zoo. Restrooms are clean, plentiful, and come equipped with changing tables.

Woodland Park Zoo

Admission: (First price is for King County residents – second price is for all other visitors.) Adults $8.50-$9.50; senior $7.75-$8.75; youth (6-17) $6.25-$7; preschool (3-5) $4.25-$4.75; toddler (0-2) free.

Season/Hours: March 15-April 30 – Daily, 9:30 a.m.-5 p.m.; May 1-Sept. 14 – Daily, 9:30 a.m. 6 p.m.; Sept. 15-Oct. 14 – Daily, 9:30 a.m. - 5 p.m.; Oct. 15-March 14 – Daily, 9:30 a.m. - 4 p.m Open 365 days a year.

Directions: From I-5 north or south, take NE 50th St. exit (#169). Go west 1.3 miles to the South Gate at N 50th St. and Fremont Ave. N. Parking lot, $3.50.

North Seattle

Places to Eat

Duke's Greenlake Chowder House

7850 Green Lake Dr. N
(206) 522-4908

Duke's Greenlake Chowder House

Hours: 11:30 a.m. - 12 a.m. (lunch and dinner).

The prow of a rowboat juts from above the front door and from that a pair of feet from an apparently snoozing fisherman. The clam chowder regularly wins awards. The well-rounded family menu offers consistently good burgers, fish and chips, pastas, and sandwiches. Duke's has the best outdoor seating of any restaurant around Green Lake.

Zeek's Pizza

7900 E Green Lake Dr. N
(206) 522-6910

Zeek's Pizza

Hours: 11 a.m. - 10 p.m.

People still think this is Guido's Pizza, but it's now Zeek's, the latest in a local chain serving some of Seattle's best and most bizarre pizza. Josephine sticks with the cheese pizza, but your older children might be bold enough to try the "Frog Belly Green" (olive and pesto) or "Thai One On" (peanut sauce, chicken, bean sprouts, etc.). The gigantic salads are winners.

The staff here, as with all the Zeek's, is young, friendly, and will make your children laugh. We like to sit at the small counter (to your left as you face the cash register) where we get a close-up look at pizzas being made. We also like critiquing the art.

Spud Fish and Chips

6860 Green Lake Way N
(206) 524-0565

Spud Fish and Chips

Hours: 11 a.m. - 9 p.m.

A regular contender for the "best fish and chips" in this city of fish and chips, Spud is better for take-out (across the street to Green Lake park) than eating in. We like the basic cod the best, although halibut, prawns, clams, and oysters are also available. This food is delivered to your hands HOT, hot enough to burn an adult's tongue, let alone a small child's – let it cool before sinking your teeth into the toothsome corn meal crust.

Rosita's Mexican Restaurant

7210 Woodlawn Ave. NE
(206) 523-3031

Rosita's Mexican Restaurant

Hours: Mon.-Thurs., 11:30 a.m. - 10 p.m.; Fri., 11:30 a.m. - 11 p.m.; Sat., 11:30 a.m. - 10:30 p.m.; Sun., 4 p.m. - 9:30 p.m.

Good basic Mexican food in a child-friendly atmosphere.

North Seattle

A Place to Shop/Rent

Gregg's Greenlake Cycle

7007 Woodlawn Ave. NE (across from Green Lake)
(206) 523-1822
www.greggscycles.com

This is a great – albeit expensive – bicycle shop, but the main reason it's in this book is that it's also a great place to rent bikes and skates for your excursions around Green Lake.

Magnolia/Queen Anne

Magnolia sits on the end of a peninsula surrounded west and south by Elliott Bay, to the north by the ship canal, and east by 15th Ave. W. The Queen Anne Hill neighborhood is perched to the west of 15th Ave. W, north of N Roy St., east of Aurora Ave. N, and south of the ship canal.

Magnolia/Queen Anne

Directions to Magnolia: From I-5 north, take the Olive/Denny exit (#166). Take Olive to Denny and turn left to cross back over the freeway. Follow Denny west. After about a mile, you will pass Seattle Center on your right. Continue on Denny until it ends at Western Ave. Turn right on Western. Western will merge onto Elliott Ave. W. Continue on Elliot (which will change into 15th Ave. W) until you see signs for the Magnolia Bridge (W Garfield St.). Follow the signs, which will take you right and then loop you back over 15th and onto the bridge. Garfield will become W Galer St. Continue straight through the 4-way stop at Howe St. Street name changes to Clisa Pl. W. Turn right onto 34th Ave. W. The next cross-street is W McGraw St., Magnolia's main drag. Free on-street parking.

Directions to Queen Anne: Directions: From I-5 north or south, take the Mercer St. exit (#167 – from I-5 north, it is a left-hand exit). Bear right onto Fairview Ave. N, then turn left onto Westlake Ave. N. Stay in the center lanes and follow the main flow of traffic as it bears left onto Broad St. N, turn right onto 5th Ave. N, then left onto N Roy St. Turn right onto Queen Anne Ave. N and continue to the top of the hill. This is the beginning of Queen Anne's main shopping strip. On-street parking, both free and metered.

Magnolia is a relatively upscale neighborhood, close to downtown, with spectacular views of Elliott Bay and the city skyline, but with a quiet, small town feel to it. Magnolia trees line the streets of the cute shopping district, but they were planted after the fact. The name is derived from early settler's misidentification of the plentiful – and also beautiful – Madrona trees.

Queen Anne is a mixed income neighborhood, featuring apartments and condominiums on its southern flank and virtual mansions as you climb the hill. The main shopping district at the top of the hill is a nice mixture of boutique shops, restaurants, and service providers.

North Seattle

Things to Do

"Pop" Mounger Pool

2535 32nd Ave. W
(206) 684-4708

This is the perfect outdoor pool for Seattle. Mounger Pool is actually two pools, heated and open from late spring through early fall, rain or shine (excepting the very rare thunderstorm).

We've had hundreds of hours of fun in the small pool. This is not a wading pool, but rather a pool built to the scale of children up to about age 6-7. Nowhere is the water depth more than about 3 feet, which means that most children over about 4 can touch the bottom everywhere, reducing your worries. Perhaps the best thing about this pool (in this city where one can't count on warm weather until July) is that it's heated to the temperature of a child's bath. Children 5 years of age and younger must meet the minimum height requirement (at least 4 feet) or must be accompanied into the pool by an adult. A minimum ratio of one adult to two children is required. On those chilly, drizzly May mornings, the sound of adults sighing "Aaaah" as they ease into the water is almost deafening. By the same token, we tend to avoid the pool on warm, sunny days – the combination of hot water, hot sun, and an extra crowded pool, can cause me to feel woozy. As far as we're concerned, this is a great cloudy day place.

The larger pool is not as warm and features a tall, twisting water slide (requires an extra fee, except during special times).

The locker rooms are new and appealing. A separate family dressing room is available.

Swimming lessons and adult programs are available, and the facility can be reserved for birthday parties.

"Pop" Mounger Pool

Cost: Adults $2.50, children/senior $1.75, infants (under 1) free.

Season/Hours: Mid-May - Mid-Sept. – Mon., 6 a.m. - 8 p.m.; Tues.-Thurs., 6 a.m. - 9 p.m; Fri., 6 a.m. - 7:30 p.m.; Sat.-Sun. & Memorial, Independence, and Labor Days, 11 a.m. - 7 p.m.

Directions: From W McGraw St., take 32nd Ave. W heading north. The pool is approximately 4 blocks north, on the left. Free parking in lot and on-street.

North Seattle

Discovery Park

3801 W Government Way
(206) 386-4236
www.ci.seattle.wa.us/parks/environment/discovparkindex.htm

courtesy Seattle Parks/Rec.

Discovery Park

At more than 500 acres, this former military installation is by far the largest park in Seattle. There is a playground near the main entrance, but don't waste your time here – there are two miles of protected tidal beaches, woods, wetlands, cliffs, and rolling meadows to explore.

We highly recommend the nature walks guided by park rangers. Call for times and to make reservations. If you have a group, a private tour tailored to your ages and interests can be arranged at a reasonable cost.

Call or check the website for details about tours and other special programs such as bird tours, tots' walks, parent/preschool adventures, beach walks, and the annual events: the Migratory Bird Festival, the Slug Festival, and the Blackberry Festival. Environmental education programs and opportunities to participate in park preservation activities might be of interest to older kids. Special school programs for K-8 are offered year-round.

Discovery Park

Hours: Dawn-dusk, daily. Visitor's Center: Daily, 8:30 a.m. - 5 p.m.; closed Christmas, New Year's Day, November 11, and Thanksgiving.

Directions: From W McGraw St., take 34th Ave. W north to W Government Way (about 1 mile). Turn left and enter the park about two blocks later. Visitor's Center and playground are just to the left as you enter.

If you want to go it on your own, stop by the visitor's center for a map. There are miles of well-maintained, relatively easy hiking trails that crisscross the entire park (know your children's limits before starting out or you'll wind up carrying them). The rocky beaches aren't for swimming – it's more of a "throw stones in to the water" and "explore nature" kind of place.

Bring binoculars if you have them – there are a lot of rare bird species here and bald eagle sightings are not at all uncommon.

For those not up to hiking, one can drive to most of the major areas of Discovery Park.

Daybreak Star Arts Center (see below) is located in the north part of the park.

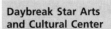

North Seattle

Daybreak Star Arts and Cultural Center

North side of Discovery Park (see above for directions)
(206) 285-4425

A project of the United Indians of All Tribes Foundation, the building built in 1977 and designed by a Colville Indian artist, is home to the Sacred Circle Gallery of American Indian Art, an interesting collection of Native American Art, both traditional (e.g., beadwork, basketry) and contemporary (e.g., painting, sculpture). If you have an interest in purchasing Indian artwork, the center hosts periodic sales throughout the fall, winter, and spring.

Each year, the center hosts more than 40,000 visitors, 10,000 of whom come for the three-day annual Pow Wow, an event featuring native dance, arts, culture and – yummiest of all – traditionally prepared salmon. Other special events are held here throughout the year.

Call for details about events and art sales.

> **Daybreak Star Arts and Cultural Center**
>
> Cost: Free
>
> Hours: Mon.-Sat, 10 a.m. - 5 p.m.; Sun., Noon - 5 p.m.

Interbay Athletic Complex

Soccer Center: 3027 17th Ave. W, (206) 283-4022
Family Golf Center: 2501 15th Ave. W (206) 285-2200

A partnership between the City of Seattle Parks and Recreation department, Interbay Family Golf Centers, and Seattle Pacific University, the complex includes a 9-hole golf course, an huge driving range, an 18-hold putting course, practice facilities, a 900 seat grass soccer stadium, baseball and softball facilities.

We're not big-time golfers, but the putting course with its waterfalls and streams is not only beautiful, but is a blast to play.

Interbay is also home to a charming community P-Patch garden.

> **Interbay Athletic Complex**
>
> Directions: As you leave downtown on 15th Ave. W, you will see the facility on the left as you approach Magnolia.

"Bhy" Kracke Park

Bigelow Ave. N and Comstock Pl.

It's not the playground (which is rudimentary) that is fun so much as it is *finding* the playground from the top of this very steep, unfortunately named park (it's pronounced "Buy Cracky," which once had a much different meaning than it does today).

The first thing you will notice is the view of the skyline from here – something for which the neighbors pay a premium. There are often joggers stretching out before or after a run.

> **"Bhy" Kracke Park**
>
> Directions: Follow directions to Queen Anne, but instead of following Queen Anne Ave. to the top of the hill, turn right onto Highland Dr. (it zigzags a bit) then bear left onto Bigelow Ave. N. Turn right onto N Comstock Pl. and park in the small 3-spot lot. If the lot is full, free on-street parking is available on Bigelow.

North Seattle

"Bhy" Kracke Park

courtesy Seattle Parks/Rec.

Children love to explore the winding walkways and lawns, lined with rhododendrons, azaleas, and seasonal plantings that wander down the hillside, playing hide-and-seek or chase.

The playground is at the bottom of the hill, which is also accessible from N 5th Ave.

There are no bathrooms, but there is, thankfully, a water fountain from which to refresh yourself after hiking back up from the "bottom" of the park.

Places to Eat

Szmania's Restaurant

3321 W McGraw Street
(206) 284-7305

> **Szmania's Restaurant**
>
> Hours: Tues.-Sat., 5 p.m. - 10 p.m.

This is a popular neighborhood restaurant that serves outstanding food AND welcomes children. The menu reinterprets German specialties using Northwest ingredients. Half-portions of many dishes are available and perfectly sized for smaller appetites. The kitchen is also open to whipping up something simple for your child. Josephine enjoys the spaetzle (small pasta-like dumplings) with or without sauce.

We prefer to sit at the kitchen counter to watch chef work in the open kitchen.

The staff is friendly – even charming.

Palisade

2601 W Marina Place (in the Elliot Bay Marina)
(206) 285-1000

> **Palisade**
>
> Hours: Mon.-Thurs., 11:30 a.m. - 2:15 p.m. & 5 p.m. - 9 p.m.; Fri., 11:30 a.m. - 2:15 p.m. & 5 p.m. - 10 p.m.; Sat., 11:30 a.m. - 2:15 p.m. & 4 p.m. - 10 p.m.; Sun., 11:30 a.m. - 2:15 p.m. & 4:30 p.m. - 9 p.m.
>
> Directions: Follow directions to Magnolia until you loop back over 15th. Just across 15th, take a slight right onto the ramp, turn left onto 23rd Ave. W, which turns into W Marina Pl.

A waterfall, tidal pools stocked with marine life, a foot bridge over the water, lush greenery, a piano player perched over the bar, a wonderful view . . . Palisade is a feast for the imagination, especially that of a small child. Unfortunately, the food isn't that great and the prices quite high. You might just want to look at the upstairs restaurant then head down to Maggie Bluffs (see below).

117

North Seattle

Maggie Bluffs

2601 W Marina Pl. (Elliott Bay Marina)
(206) 283-8322

Not as pretty to look at as her expensive upstairs partner Palisade (see above), but with a menu better suited to a child's taste (burgers, pizza, pasta) and a limited pocketbook. The view is through the masts of the boats in the marina, but still nice.

5 Spot Café

1502 Queen Anne Ave. N (at W Galer)
(206) 285-7768
www.chowfoods.com/5-spot.asp

This is a popular, tasty restaurant for breakfast, lunch, or dinner. You will have no problem feeding your children from the extensive kid's menu. The great bonus here is that the food for the adult palate is not "dumbed down" to bring in families. There are both comfort foods on the menu (like meat and mashed potatoes) as well as more exotic fare (as emphasized by the restaurant's tackling of various American regional cuisines on a rotational basis).

Definitely leave room for dessert.

Crayons and toys are usually available for the kids.

"Chain" restaurant outlets in the area that are mentioned elsewhere

Pizzeria Pagliacci, 550 Queen Anne Ave. N, (206) 285-1232

Zeek's Pizza, 41 Dravus St., (206) 285-6046

Pasta & Co., 2109 Queen Anne Ave. N, (206) 283-1182

Maggie Bluffs

Hours:
Mon.-Thurs., 11:30 a.m. - 9 p.m.;
Fri., 11:30 a.m. - 9:30 p.m.;
Sat., 8:30 a.m. - 9:30 p.m.;
Sun., 8:30 a.m. - 9 p.m.

Directions: See directions to Palisade (above).

5 Spot Café

Hours:
Mon.-Fri., 8:30 a.m. - 12 a.m.;
Sat.-Sun., 8:30 a.m. - 3 p.m. & 5 p.m. - 12 a.m..

Directions: (Follow directions to Queen Anne.) The restaurant (under a neon coffee cup) will be on your right just after crossing W Galer St.

North Seattle

Wallingford

Bordered by Stone Way to the west, I-5 to the east, N 50th St. to the north, and Lake Union to the south.

Wallingford

Directions: From I-5 north or south, take exit 169 (N 45th St.) and head west on N 45th. You're in Wallingford once you're west of I-5, although you should drive a few blocks farther to get to the heart of the neighborhood. On-street parking.

This middle-class family neighborhood with its "Main Street" (N 45th St.) of mom & pop retailers and restaurants would feel like small-town America if not for the horrendous east-west traffic. Wallingford's homey feel and adjacency to Green Lake, the Woodland Park Zoo, Lake Union, Fremont, and the University of Washington makes it a popular residential area for young families. We know many people who live here who rarely venture beyond walking distance of their homes.

Things to Do

Meridan Playground

NE 50th St. and Meridian Ave. N

We like this park because it is both spacious and protected from the busy streets surrounding it by high fences and lush shrubbery, giving it a secure, pastoral feeling in the midst of the city. You can let your children roam around the grassy lawn, planted with flowering trees (in the spring) without losing sight of them or worrying they will stumble into traffic. As we went to press, the playground area was in the midst of a major overhaul. We usually bring balls, bats, and other sports equipment. During the school year you will be sharing the playground with students from the private Meridian School located within the park grounds.

Wallingford Playfield

Wallingford Ave. N and N 42nd St.

courtesy Seattle Parks/Rec.

Wallingford Playfield

We've spent hundreds of hours in this park, mainly because Josephine's preschool was nearby, and it was an easy place to meet friends after school. The popular wading pool is small and the playground equipment aging, but a major overhaul of the park was in process at the time of publication. Our friend Elly says this park is her favorite place to ride her bike – she especially likes tearing down the grassy hills.

North Seattle

Gas Works Park

N Northlake Way on Lake Union

One of the most unusual parks you will find anywhere, the 20 acre site was originally cleared in 1906 to construct a plant to manufacture synthetic gas from coal, and later, oil. The boiler house and other gears, pistons and various other parts of the obsolete plant remain today – graffiti covered – as a kind of industrial-era landscape/sculpture. While children are not allowed to climb on the old machinery, they are still fascinated with exploring this Rube Goldberg-esque maze, which is now a covered "play barn." For those with an interest, signage explains the former function of the equipment. The playground features slides, poles, sand, and a climbing structure. The views are outstanding, offering the downtown skyline across Lake Union, a fantastic peek at the Eastlake houseboats of *Sleepless in Seattle* (the movie) fame, and a good look back at the Aurora and Fremont bridges spanning the ship canal. This is a great place from which to watch the float planes take-off and land and a very popular spot from which to take-in the fireworks on the Fourth of July. There is no better place to fly and kite. Climb up the winding path to the top of the hill for a 360-degree vantage point and the huge art-sundial. Running and rolling back down the steep slopes is a favorite activity. Cyclists and skaters like to park in the large lot and access the Burke-Gilman trail from here.

On Tuesday evenings from late spring through early fall, you may notice all manner of sailing vessels in the waters of Lake Union, taking part in the informal and highly goofy "Duck Dodge" race. You can rent a boat at Sailboat Rentals and Yacht Charters (below) and take part if you wish.

Places to Eat

The Jitterbug

2114 N 45th St.
(206) 547-6313

The Jitterbug
Hours: Daily, 8 a.m. - 10 p.m.

Josephine's friend Elly calls this her favorite restaurant. For breakfast, lunch, or dinner, the Jitterbug serves a varied adult menu that borders on the exotic and experimental at times, while the extensive kid's menu features all the things children like best (pastas, sandwiches, quesadillas, burgers, waffles, pancakes, etc.). The staff love their young customers. Crayons and dimestore style toys are part of the standard service. We like to sit at the counter to watch the cooks work, but pay attention – I was once distracted by a waiter while one of the kitchen staff secretly served Josephine a scoop of vanilla ice cream (gratis). Prices tend to be a bit high.

North Seattle

Egg Cetera's Blue Star Cafe

4512 Stone Way N
(206) 548-0345

Egg Cetera's Blue Star Cafe

Hours: Mon.-Thurs., 7 a.m. - 3 p.m.
& 5 p.m. - 10 p.m.; Fri., 7 a.m. - 3 p.m.
& 5 p.m. - 11 p.m.; Sat., 8 a.m. - 3 p.m.
& 5 p.m. - 11 p.m.; Sun., 8 a.m. - 3 p.m.
& 5 p.m.- 10 p.m.

A casual, laid-back joint, many people think of this as a place to drink beer – and it is – but it's also a great place for a meal with children. The breakfast menu features eggs, eggs, and eggs. Lunch is all about burgers and sandwiches. Dinnertime tends to be oriented more toward the bar area. Service can be slow. Ask for a coloring book (although they don't always have one).

Julia's

4401 Wallingford Ave. N
(206) 633-1175

Julia's

Hours: Mon., 7 a.m. - 3 p.m.;
Tues.-Wed., 7 a.m. - 9 p.m.;
Thurs.-Sat., 7 a.m. - 10 p.m.;
Sun., 7 a.m. - 9 p.m.

If Julia's didn't invent brunch in Seattle, it is certainly one of the early pioneers. The food is generally excellent – people rave about the French toast. I'm relying on second-hand information for brunch, however, given that Josephine simply can't handle the interminable wait on Sunday morning. The lunch menu is simple and solid, with tasty vegetarian options available.

University District/Sand Point

The area described here lies east of I-5, is bordered on the south by Portage and Union Bays, the east by Lake Washington, and north by NE 75th.

The University of Washington is one of the largest and most highly-regarded public institutions of higher learning in the U.S. On the other hand, I've known dozens of graduates who chose the school based almost exclusively on the tour of the beautiful campus. As you would expect from September through June, the streets of the "U-District" are crowded with students, most of whom are on their own for the first time – their attire and behavior often destined to be something to look back on with embarrassment.

"The Ave" (University Avenue) is the heart of off-campus activities, lined with bars, cheap

University District/Sand Point

Directions: From I-5 north or south, take 45th Street exit (#169). Follow 45th east to University Ave. Metered on-street parking and pay lots.

To get to the Univ. of Wash. Campus, continue on 45th to 17th Ave. and turn right. You must pay to park on campus. You will need $7 to enter campus and a destination in mind (I usually say I'm going to the Burke Museum). If you park less than 4 hours, you will receive some of your $7 back, depending on how long you parked.

To get to the University Village, Ravenna, Laurelhurst, or Sand Point, you will continue on 45th. See below for specific directions for each destination.

North Seattle

restaurants, and good used bookstores. Josephine and I don't really spend a lot of time here, mainly because of all the panhandlers, some of whom are staggeringly drunk. My personal strategy is to just smile, make eye contact and say "Not today," but with a child, the element of danger makes it more significant than just a hassle.

Shoppers (as opposed to students) have moved during the past decade farther east and into the University Village (see below) located on the other side of campus.

What I'm calling Sand Point includes the upscale enclaves of Laurelhurst and Windermere, and several middle class neighborhoods, including Ravenna, University Village, Hawthorne Hills, and View Ridge.

Things to Do

University of Washington

15th Ave. NE and NE 45th St.
Visitors Information Center: 4014 University Way NE
(206) 543-9198
www.washington.edu/univrel/visitors/

Walking the campus is a favorite autumn (for the fall colors) or springtime (for the flowering trees, especially the cherries) walk. We like to just wander around admiring the landscaping and architecture, but for those seeking a more purposeful experience, the Visitors Information Center offers 90-minute, guided walking tours on weekdays at 10:30 a.m. The campus grounds are relatively flat, but I wouldn't recommend this for small children. As an alternative, you can pick-up an excellent self-guided walking tour brochure from the Visitor's Center (also downloadable from the website). This is really a fun way to see campus – you know what you're looking at while maintaining the flexibility so desirable when dealing with the caprices of young children.

The UW offers a variety of educational and entertainment opportunities for families, ranging from theater and music to athletics and . . . well, education.

The Burke Museum of Natural History and Culture (see below) is here, as is the Henry Art Gallery (see below). Washington's intercollegiate sports program is top-notch and a lot more than just a vaunted football powerhouse. The UW annually sponsors hundreds of concerts, conferences, dance and drama performances, exhibits, films, lectures, operas, readings, and workshops, all open to the public.

North Seattle

Meany Theater

4001 University Way NE
(206) 543-4880
(800) 859-5342 (outside Seattle)

A venue for both students and visiting artists, Meany Theater offers a wide range of musical, dramatic and dance performances, many of which would be appropriate for children capable of sitting through an entire performance. Check the website or call for information about specific performances.

Burke Museum of Natural History and Culture

UW Campus (enter at 17th Ave. from NE 45th – museum is just inside campus to the right)
Mailing address: Box 353010
University of Washington
(206) 543-5591
(206) 543-5590 (24-hour recorded message)
www.washington.edu/burkemuseum

Burke Museum of Natural History and Culture

Cost: Adult $8; seniors $6.50; students $5; children under 5 are free

Hours: Daily, 10 a.m. - 5 p.m.; Thurs. until 8 p.m. Closed Independence Day, Thanksgiving Day, Christmas Day, New Year's Day.

If you're visiting from New York, you might think the Burke no great shakes, but it is a fascinating, educational place and its smaller scale makes it more accessible to young children. Naturally, the dinosaur and other prehistoric skeletons will be the focus for most children. The skeletons are nicely displayed in a gallery, which includes fossils, a walk-through volcano, and many exhibits designed to enrich the experience of viewing "old bones."

The "Discovery Center" is a hands-on area where children can examine fossils with their fingers as well as large magnifiers, observe a real seismograph (one of our first stops after the 2000 quake was to check out the records here), work puzzles, play games and use geological tools, and operate a giant periscope that peeks in at the dinosaurs in the next gallery (when Josephine was little and afraid of the skeletons, this was the only way she felt safe viewing them).

At the front desk, each child receives a "passport" (if you don't, ask for one), which they "stamp" at special stations located throughout the main level exhibits. It seems like a silly, little thing, but Josephine and her friends get a kick out of it.

The "culture" aspect of the museum's mission is achieved by special exhibits in the upstairs gallery and by the permanent "Pacific Voices" display downstairs. Visitors learn about the various Pacific Rim cultures through the standard displays of relics, costumes, and dioramas. What we enjoy here is seeking out the "hidden" drawers located in the bases of many of the display cases. Inside, we

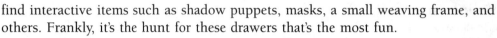

North Seattle

find interactive items such as shadow puppets, masks, a small weaving frame, and others. Frankly, it's the hunt for these drawers that's the most fun.

Special weekend children's activities take place throughout the year. Call for information about this and the guided tours for children.

The Burke is available for private events. Ask about Dinosaur Birthday Parties: (206) 221-2853.

Burke-Gilman/Sammamish Trail
Runs from Fremont to Redmond (accessible from the east edge of campus)

The entry for the Burke-Gilman Trail could have been included in any one of a half-dozen sections of this book, covering as it does some 28-miles from Fremont to Redmond. I've chosen to put it here because the U-District section of the trail is probably the most heavily used part of the entire length, due to its popularity with students and faculty peddling to class.

It's paved, relatively flat, impeccably maintained, and appropriate for cycling, skating, walking, or jogging.

For the most part, Burke-Gilman is separated from traffic, but it does cross busy streets, so you can't exactly let the tykes freewheel it the whole way, and there are places and times (such as just before or after a Husky home football game) when the trail is almost too busy for bikes.

courtesy Seattle Parks/Rec.

Burke-Gilman/Sammamish Trail

King County's RoadShare Program has an excellent free map of all the bike trails in the county, including this one. You may order one by calling (206) 263-4729 or 263-4788, via the Internet at **www.metrokc.gov/kcdot/tp/bike/bikemap.htm**, or by writing to: King County RoadShare Program, Transportation Planning Division, Dept. of Transportation, 201 S Jackson St., MS KSC-TR-0813, Seattle, WA 98104-3856.

North Seattle

Medicinal Herb Garden

UW Campus (on Stevens Way across from the Botany greenhouse and Anderson Hall)
Mailing Address: Friends of the Medicinal Herb Garden
c/o Botany Department
University of Washington
Box 355325
Seattle, WA 98195-5325
(206) 543-1126
www.nnlm.gov/pnr/uwmhg/

This is a neat, cozy garden containing hundreds of species of plants with medicinal properties. In the spring and summer, these tidy gravel paths and well-maintained beds are charming – everything is left to get wilder during the fall and winter. We like to (gently) rub the leaves of herbs and other plants with our fingers to carry their scent with us when we leave.

The Botany greenhouse across the street is open to the public, although the hours are irregular.

Henry Art Gallery

15th Ave. NE and NE 41st St. (UW Campus, west side)
(206) 543-2280
www.henryart.org

Henry Art Gallery

Cost: Adults $6; seniors $4.50; students (w/ID) and children under 13 are free.

Hours: Tues.-Sun., 11 a.m. - 5 p.m.; Thurs., until 8 p.m. Closed July 4, Thanksgiving, Christmas Eve and Day, New Year's Day. Café closes 30 minutes before museum.

The Henry Art Gallery focuses on modern and contemporary art and, as such, exhibits artworks as brilliant and soulful as they are bizarre and unsettling. Of course, it's always fascinating to compare adult perceptions with those of a child, and nothing elicits differences like modern art.

I'll never forget one disturbing piece of video art that was part of a temporary exhibit. It involved a woman who appeared to be trapped inside a series of television sets, mouthing nonsequiters. The adults in our group were repulsed, almost unable to even look at it. Josephine, on the other hand, thought it was hilarious – she kept dragging us back to laugh at it. After a while, we all started laughing. I don't know if she understood the piece better than we did, but I like her interpretation better than ours.

The museum is new and bright. My only complaint is that voices echo mightily. I feel like I'm constantly hushing Josephine.

The food in the café isn't bad.

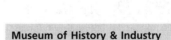

North Seattle

Museum of History & Industry

2700 24th Ave. E
(206) 324-1126
www.seattlehistory.org

MOHAI ("Mow-hi"), as it is called locally, opened its doors in 1952 with the mission of preserving, collecting, and presenting the history of the Pacific Northwest. The museum's collections include everything from parts of ships to period clothing, technology, and tools from the earliest days of Seattle.

> **Museum of History & Industry**
>
> Cost: Adults $5.50; seniors/youth (ages 6-12) $3; preschoolers (ages 2-5) $1; under 2 are free.
>
> Hours: Daily, 10 a.m. - 5 p.m. Closed Thanksgiving and Christmas.
>
> Directions: From Interstate 5 take State Route 520 (exit 168B); exit at Montlake Boulevard; go through stoplight one block to 24th Avenue East. Turn left into the museum's driveway. Follow road to parking lot. Free parking.

Josephine loves the "Seattle in the 1880s" exhibit which features a street of shops like those that might have been found in the area during the latter part of the 19th century, including a saloon, blacksmith, barber shop, and bank. She also enjoys the display of ship figureheads and MOHAI's clothing collection. Older children might appreciate learning about the history of the region's vital salmon fisheries and fish processing industry.

Guided tours are offered daily and frequent special weekend family programs are a great way for families to explore dance, music, storytelling, and crafts that help bring history to life. Call for details.

If you need to get outside after a visit to the museum, just head across the parking lot and down toward Lake Washington where you will find the western end of the Washington Park Arboretum's Waterfront Trail (see pp.156 for more information). Pick up a brochure at MOHAI and take yourselves on a self-guided tour of Seattle's largest wetlands.

University of Washington Intercollegiate Athletics

Mailing address: University of Washington Department of Athletics
Graves Building, Box 354070
Seattle, WA 98195-4070
(206) 616-9227 (for tour)
(206) 543-2200 (ticket office)
www.gohuskies.fansonly.com (for ticket and schedule info.)
www.depts.washington.edu/phearts/tours/ (for tour info.)

U of W Athletics is one of the top intercollegiate programs in the country. Fall through spring, there is almost always some sporting event taking place, often involving nationally-ranked teams. Check the website or call the ticket office for information. While the men's football team (plays in the fall) is the most popular

North Seattle

program, we highly recommend sports such as women's basketball, soccer and softball, as well as men's and women's crew, all of which are perennial national powerhouses.

If you're interested in a first-hand view of the university's athletic facilities, tours are available. Your sports fan will love the inside look at Husky Stadium and Hec Edmundson Pavilion, as well as the baseball, softball, and soccer stadiums. These free tours must be scheduled a minimum of 2 weeks in advance and take about an hour.

University of Washington Waterfront Activity Center

**Located directly behind Husky Stadium (Montlake Blvd.) on Union Bay and the Montlake Cut. The entrance for visitor parking is found north of Husky Stadium on Montlake Blvd.
(206) 543-9433**

University of Washington Waterfront Activity Center

Canoe and rowboat rentals: $6.50 per hour.

Hours: Boat Rentals – Daily, dawn - dusk (no rentals Nov.-Jan. and during football games). Building hours: Sept. – Daily, 10 a.m. - 8 p.m.; Oct. – Daily, 10 a.m. - 7 p.m.; Nov.-Dec. – Daily, 10 a.m. - 5 p.m.

Push off in your own canoe or rowboat to explore the Montlake Cut, Union Bay, Lake Washington, Foster Island, and the waterways in and around the arboretum. Although the plant and animal life is fascinating, the real kick for us is tooling around and under the state highway 520 floating bridge.

Life jackets are provided, although they have nothing suitable for children weighing under 25 pounds.

University of Washington Campus Public Observatory

**U of W campus (NE 45th St. & 17th Ave. NE, east of the Burke Museum)
(206) 543-0126 (leave message)
www.astro.washington.edu/observatory**

University of Washington Campus Public Observatory

Cost: Free

Hours: Varies by season, call first.

Housing one of the oldest working telescopes in the West, the observatory is home to an antique telescope that still delivers clear images of the moon, planets, and other astronomical objects. Scientific research is no longer performed from this facility, which is operated by a tour guide on a volunteer basis.

North Seattle

University Village

Located at the cross roads of 45th Ave. NE and 25th Ave. (east of U of W campus)
(206) 523-0622
www.uvillage.com

I've tried to stay away from shopping centers in this book, largely due to my belief that they are all essentially the same, but the University Village is one of the most child-filled places in the city. Its attraction, frankly, eludes me, but we find ourselves here with an alarming regularity.

You will find many of the usual suspects as far as large retailers (e.g., The Gap, Barnes & Noble, Abercrombie & Fitch, The Pottery Barn) plus some interesting smaller concerns (e.g., The Blue Canoe, Pasta & Co., Ravenna Gardens).

University Village

Directions: From the I-5 corridor, take the 520 East junction and then exit using the Montlake Blvd. exit. Turn left onto Montlake and cross the drawbridge. Continue forward through two traffic lights, passing Husky Stadium on your right. Follow Montlake until you see signs for 25th Avenue NE. Turn slightly left onto 25th and follow the signs to University Village.

There is a small playground intended for children 6 and under, that we call the "Law of the Jungle Playground." The central attraction is the half-dozen or so toy cars and trucks: there are almost always more children wanting to drive them than there are vehicles. Older kids patrol the enclosed space waiting for a car to be abandoned, then rush pell-mell to claim it. When it's crowded (and it often is) there is nearly always at least one child in tears over being beaten-out. The play structure is minimal, and although the ground is paved with a soft, rubberized surface, parents hover around it trying to prevent their toddlers from falling off. In the winter, the playground is windy, cold, and only partially protected from the rain – in the summer, it's somehow the hottest place on earth. So, why is this place so popular? Because if shoppers with children come in groups, one adult can monitor the children, who are at least fenced-in, while the other grown-ups shop.

If you have grocery shopping to do, the large QFC supermarket (which is the only one in the local chain that doesn't seem to have deteriorated under Kroger's ownership) has a very tiny, yet fun, childcare area, staffed with a bright, cheery team of caretakers. They have no television and entertain the children with arts, crafts, and games. Josephine and her friends actually request that we shop here. Making this extra attractive for parents is the in-store "lounge" area, complete with comfortable chairs, a fireplace, newsstand, and several "shops" from which you can get snacks and beverages. I am not the only one who has taken a novel with me and used the facility for a break in the middle of a hectic day.

North Seattle

The Barnes & Noble children's books area is also a place to linger. We try not to abuse their patience, but we love to snuggle up in one of the big, comfy chairs and read. The story times take place on a cute little stage where Josephine likes to "perform" when it's not in use for official purposes. Call (206) 517-4107 for a schedule of events.

There are three fountains in the Village that are fun for wishing and splashing fingers. On hot days, children take off their shoes and play in the large one in the north part of the campus near Ravenna Gardens – it's not officially permitted, but I've never known anyone to be kicked out.

Paint the Town (206-527-8554) sells pottery items (e.g., mugs, plats, containers, figurines) that you and your child paint and then leave to be glazed. It's fun and the finished products make great gifts.

If your child needs a haircut, the toy store Kid's Club recently added a barbershop that caters exclusively to children.

The Village is home to dozens of dining options, none of which is spectacular from a gustatory perspective (except maybe the Pasta & Co. take-out deli), but they *all* are child-friendly.

Laurelhurst Playground and Community Center

4554 NE 41st St.
(206) 684-7531
www.ci.seattle.wa.us/seattle/parks/Centers/Laurelcc.htm

Laurelhurst Playground and Community Center

Hours: Mon.-Fri., 9 a.m. - 8 p.m.

Directions: Continue on NE 45th St. past the University Village. Don't bear left onto Sand Point Way (which will be the natural tendency), but stay right on NE 45th. Turn right onto 41st Ave. NE, then left onto NE 41st St. The entrance to the playground is on your left.

The play structures are large, safe, and set into a bed of deep, soft sand. In spite of being surrounded by a residential neighborhood, it is rarely crowded. You will find baseball/softball diamonds and acres of grassy fields in which to run

The community center's signature event is its annual Salmon Bake, which is usually held on the last Wednesday in July. Toddler and young children's activities take place throughout the year. Saturday night roller-skating in the gym.

North Seattle

Sand Point Magnuson Park

7400 Sand Point Way NE
(206) 684-4946
www.ci.seattle.wa.us/seattle/parks/parkspaces/spmagnuson.htm

Most of our visits here are to the new Junior League Playground (enter at NE 74th St.) – for our money, the best pure playground in the city. There is not one, not two, but three separate play structures, a cool playhouse, plentiful swings, and a sandbox with toys. The lawn is large enough for sports activities and the "wild" meadow area has enough nature in it to occupy your little naturalists. The giant parking lot is somewhat separated from the play area, making your traffic concerns minimal. The best part is that a parent can see the entire playground from just about anywhere, removing much of the stress out of minding several children at once.

The worst part is that bathroom facilities at the playground are limited to a pair of portable toilets, which aren't usually filthy, but they aren't exactly appealing either. We generally opt to use the bushes.

> **Sand Point Magnuson Park**
>
> Directions: From Interstate 5, take the NE 45th Street exit, go east on 45th, past the University of Washington, and down the 45th Street ramp as it merges into Sand Point Way NE. Follow Sand Point Way eastward. As the street begins to curve northward, the entrances to Sand Point Magnuson Park will be on your right at NE 65th Street and NE 74th Street.
>
> Hours: May 1-Labor Day - Daily, 4 a.m. - 11:30 p.m.; After Labor Day-April 30 – Daily, 4 a.m. - 10 p.m.

courtesy Seattle Parks/Rec.

Sand Point Magnuson Park

Although you can walk from the playground to the shores of Lake Washington, those with very short-legged companions might want to drive south, then east to the shoreline parking lots (or enter at NE 65th St.). Here you will find the swimming beach, a tiny wading pool, and real restrooms (open during summer only). The Lake Shore Promenade is a paved trail that follows the water's edge. You will find several interesting vestiges of the park's past as a naval station to ponder over, as well as artwork such as the pod of nearly two dozen Orca whale fins that protrude from the turf, made from the wings of decommissioned military aircraft. Kite Hill – not surprisingly – is a fabulous place from which to send your wings-on-strings soaring.

The Magnuson Park complex includes sports fields, tennis courts, a boat launch, residences (in the former barracks), and the slow influx of small businesses and organizations.

Dozens of special events (such as the Seattle Public Library book sales, garden shows, and musical performances) are held here each year. Call or check the website for a schedule of events.

North Seattle

NOAA Western Regional Center

7600 Sand Point Way NE
(206) 526-6026
www.wasc.noaa.gov

NOAA Western Regional Center

Cost: Free

Hours: Daily, 5 a.m. – 7 p.m.

Directions: From Interstate 5, take the NE 45th Street exit, go east on 45th, past the University of Washington, and down the 45th Street ramp as it merges into Sand Point Way NE. Follow Sand Point Way eastward, then north. The entrance to NOAA is on your right at about NE 75th St. (it looks like another military installation). Free parking in lot.

NOAA's (National Oceanographic and Atmospheric Administration) art walk is an alternative for families who want to admire art without being confined by the walls and rules of a traditional museum.

Park in the northwest corner of the parking lot where you will find artist Martin Puryear's "Knoll for NOAA." As you continue along the paved waterfront walkway, you will discover other large works of art, including the beloved "A Sound Garden" by Doug Hollis. This sculpture (the namesake of the "grunge" musical act) contains aluminum tubing that acts like woodwind instruments when the wind blows, creating "music" of a spooky variety. It's a short, easy walk – strollers and small children should have no trouble.

The Modern Day Café is located in Building 2 and serves breakfast and lunch on weekdays from 6 a.m. to 4 p.m. (206-523-3719).

Matthew's Beach

NE 93rd St. at Sand Point Way NE

Matthew's Beach

Hours: Daily, 4 a.m. - 11:30 p.m.

Directions: From Interstate 5, take the NE 45th Street exit, go east on 45th, past the University of Washington, and down the 45th Street ramp as it merges into Sand Point Way NE. Follow Sand Point Way eastward then north. The entrance to Matthews Beach is on your right at NE 93rd St. Free parking in lot, although it can be full on sunny afternoons.

We're not as excited about this, Seattle's largest freshwater beach, as some people we know, but it is very popular in the summer. Lifeguards patrol this sand and grass swimming area during the summer. Bathrooms and showers are available.

Winding walking trails curve around the grounds, connecting with Burke-Gilman Trail (see above). Watch out for speeding bikes.

The playground is better than average and includes one of those big, "curly" slides to which Josephine is partial. The equipment is varied enough to offer something for all ages, which makes it a good place to take groups of mixed-aged children.

The parking lot gets full on warm afternoons, and watch out for goose poop!

North Seattle

Ravenna Park

5520 Ravenna Ave.
www.ci.seattle.wa.us/parks/parkspaces/ravenna.htm

This is a great place to introduce tots to the joys of hiking. The 1/2 mile wooded trail cuts through a fir and cedar wooded ravine that connects two picnic areas. It's flat, easy going.

The wading pool is filled and chlorinated daily during summer months. It's a great reward after such a "long" hike.

A Place to Shop

All for Kids Books & Music

2900 NE Blakeley St.
(206) 526-2768

If there is a better children's bookstore in Seattle, we've yet to find it. The selection is astounding, and the staff seems to know the contents of every book in the place.

When Josephine is dealing with a particular social or emotional issue, we like to find a book that will help our family talk about it. On a recent visit I gave the woman at the register my daughter's age and described the problem she was having understanding certain subtleties of "friendship." I was taken to the store's "feelings" section where I was left to peruse the titles, while two employees began pulling fiction titles that "happen to deal with the issue." Within minutes I had a half-dozen books from which to choose. But it didn't stop there: I was then informed that some parents don't like one of the titles because the characters speak "kindergartenese", warned that another might be a little "old" for Josephine, and given plot synopses of all the books in my arms. The cherry on this cake of impromptu parent education was helpful suggestions on how to *use* the generalities in the books to focus on our specific issue. Wow!

All for Kids carries music and a few toys as well, but the books are the focus. Story time is usually at 10:30 a.m. on Tuesdays, but you might want to confirm by phone first.

Ravenna Park

Hours: Daily, 4 a.m. - 11:30 p.m.

Directions: From I-5 north, take the NE 65th St. exit. Turn right on to Ravenna Blvd. to 20th Avenue NE. Turn left on 20th Avenue NE. The parking lot is on the right hand side of the street on the corner of NE 58th St. and 20th Avenue NE. From I-5 south, take the N 85th St./NE 80th St. exit. Follow the sign to NE 80th St. Go east on NE 80th St. to 15th Avenue NE. Turn right on to 15th Avenue NE to Ravenna Blvd. Turn left on to Ravenna Blvd. Take Ravenna Blvd. to 20th Avenue NE. Turn left on 20th Avenue NE. The parking lot is on the right hand side of the street on the corner of NE 58th St. and 20th Avenue NE.

All for Kids Books & Music

Hours:
Mon-Sat 10 a.m. - 6 p.m.,
Sun 12 p.m. - 5 p.m.

Directions: (See directions to University Village above.) Continue on 25th Ave. NE past the University Village. Turn right on NE Blakeley St. All for Kids will be on your left. Free parking in front of store.

North Seattle

Other North Seattle Things to Do

Northwest Puppet Center

9123 15th Ave. NE
(206) 523-2579
www.nwpuppet.org

Northwest Puppet Center

Cost: Adults $8.50, children $6.50. Season passes available.

Season/Hours: October through April. Call ahead or check website for showtimes

Directions: Going north on I-5, take the Lake City Way Exit #171. Turn left at 15th Ave. NE and continue to 92nd St. Theater will be your left. Going south on I-5, take the Northgate exit #173 and go east on Northgate Way to 15th Ave. NE. Turn right on 15th Ave. NE and go straight until 92nd St. Theater will be on your right. Free on-street parking, but remember this is a residential neighborhood, so don't block driveways.

Home of the Carter Family Marionettes – resident company of internationally acclaimed puppeteers Chris and Steven Carter – the NWPC stages over 250 performances a year in a charmingly renovated church-turned-theater in the Maple Leaf neighborhood of Seattle. We have been enthusiastic NWPC season-ticket holders since Josephine was 2-years-old.

The repertoire includes both traditional fairy tales and contemporary adaptations, often liberally spiced with hilarious modernizations and live music. Guest productions are imported from all over the world, including puppet masters from Europe, Asia, South America, and Africa. And since the cost is moderate (especially with a Puppet-Pass), it's possible to see favorite productions more than once, as Josephine often requests.

Children are encouraged to sit on the carpeted floor in front of the stage, but are expected to behave appropriately. This doesn't, however, mean absolute silence – many performers demand audience participation. The theater store offers a wonderful selection of reasonably priced puppets and accessories. Snacks are also available.

We like to arrive early to burn-off any excess energy on the small NWPC playground (with a covered picnic area) located outside the theater.

Birthday parties at NWPC are a fun way to celebrate. The museum area may be rented by the hour for a nominal fee, and the friendly staff provides gratis invitations in advance, and sets up tables in the lobby for cake and ice cream (which you provide) after the show. You may also purchase party favors, including puppets, for each child to take home. The biggest attraction for Josephine, however, was that she got to wear a birthday-crown, stand on the stage, and be serenaded by the entire audience singing "Happy Birthday"!

North Seattle

Carkeek Park

950 NW Carkeek Park Rd.
(206) 684-0877
www.ci.seattle.wa.us/parks/parkspaces/Carkeek.htm

A favorite north end beach park, with 216-acres of wooded trails, a salmon stream (Pipers Creek), and a playground built around a giant salmon tunnel slide. What we particularly like about this park is that the grassy playground area is separated from the sandy beach by a parking lot and a short hike over a pedestrian bridge, under which trains regularly pass. This allows us to eat our picnic lunch *before* heading to the water, thus avoiding the upset of sand in the peanut butter.

On cooler days, easy hiking trails, playground equipment, an archery range (bring your own gear), train-watching, and Olympic Mountain views are plenty, but when it's warm, you'll be dragged to the beach. The creek that empties into Puget Sound from under the railroad tracks is the most popular play area. Often, it's deep enough to ride floatation devices in the current. This part of the beach is pretty rocky – you'll probably have more fun with water sandals/shoes. It is possible for a child to climb up to the railroad tracks, so stay on your toes.

Bathrooms are near the playground, so make sure everyone's had their chance before heading out on a hike or down to the beach.

The Carkeek Park Environmental Education Center offers free and low cost environmental education classes for children and adults. Call for details.

> **Carkeek Park**
>
> Hours: Daily, 6 a.m. - 10 p.m.
>
> Directions: From I-5, take the Northgate exit and go west on Northgate Way. Cross the intersections of Meridian and Aurora. Continue westbound to Greenwood Avenue N. Turn right (north) onto Greenwood. Drive 2 blocks to NW 110th. Turn left (west) onto NW 110th Street. Cross 3rd Avenue NW and continue as 110th becomes Carkeek Park Road. The park entrance is on the left at the valley's low point on the road. Once inside the park, take an immediate right for the Education Center or continue straight ahead for the trails, play, and picnic areas and Carkeek beach.

Bitter Lake Community Center

13035 Linden Ave. N
(206) 684-7524
www.ci.seattle.wa.us/parks/Centers/Bitterlk.htm

This is a brand, spankin' new City of Seattle facility with a full-sized gym and tons of family activities, including morning and afternoon preschool, childcare (for grades K-5), sports, music, arts, and cooking programs for toddlers, school-aged children, teens, adults, and seniors. The schedules and specific programs vary by season and some require pre-registration. Prices tend to be reasonable.

> **Bitter Lake Community Center**
>
> Hours: Mon.-Fri., 9 a.m. - 9:30 p.m.; Sat., 9 a.m. - 5 p.m..; Sun., 12 p.m. - 4 p.m.; Closed major holidays.
>
> Directions: From I-5, take exit #174 and head west on N 130th St. to Linden Avenue N. The community center is located on the northwest corner of Linden and 130th.

North Seattle

The drop-in programs are great for rainy days. The "Toddler Open Gym," for instance, features age-appropriate toys and equipment in a safe, self-contained space. Friday nights from 6:30 p.m. - 8:15 p.m. are "Family Skate Nights" (after 8:15 p.m. is set aside for teenaged skaters). Bring your own skates or use the ones provided. At $2 per person, it's a great deal. On Saturday afternoons from 11 p.m. - 2 p.m., families gather in the art room to paint pieces of pottery (e.g., mugs, bowls, plates) which are then fired and ready for pick-up the following Saturday (prices per piece range from $5-$8). Call or check the website for seasonal activities and to confirm times.

Facility is available for birthday parties and other events.

The Bitter Lake Family Center is housed within this facility (see below).

Bitter Lake Family Center

13035 Linden Ave. N
(206) 368-0172

Bitter Lake Family Center

Hours: Mon.-Fri., 9 a.m. - 9:30 p.m.; Sat., 9 a.m. - 5 p.m..; Sun., 12 p.m. - 4 p.m.; Closed major holidays.

Directions: From I-5, take exit #174 and head west on N 130th St. to Linden Avenue N. The Family Center is located within the Bitter Lake Community Center, which is located on the northwest corner of Linden and 130th.

The Family Center offers a variety of parent education and related classes and workshops at reasonable prices. Recent offerings included a workshop on protecting children from being abducted/molested, a class on dealing with destructive adolescent behavior, and a free series on parenting preschoolers.

Low-cost and free seasonal events for families are also hosted by the Family Center. Recent offerings included "Dinner and a Movie" for $1 per person, a "Peace Celebration," a free ice cream social, and a "Tropical Winter Get-Away" to an imaginary tropical island, including music, stories, and treats. These are popular activities and require registration. Call for current events, costs, and times.

Finally, the Family Center hosts free drop-in play times for parents and toddlers in their well-equipped Children's Room. Call for schedule.

North Seattle

Helene Madison Pool

13401 Meridian Ave. N
(206) 684-4979

This nice, warm (85°), indoor pool offers swimming lessons (group and individual) and special "Family Swim" times. Children under 3' 8" must be accompanied by an adult. Flotation toys are allowed only in the shallow end. Call for schedule or to find out about using the facility for a party.

> **Helene Madison Pool**
>
> Recreational swim fees: Adults $2.50, children (1-18) $1.75, under 1 free.
>
> Hours: Mon.-Fri., 12 p.m. - 8 p.m.; Sun., 10 a.m. - 6 p.m.; Closed Sat., major holidays, and for swim meets.

A Place to Shop

Top Ten Toys

104 N 85th Street
(206) 782-0098

This is my favorite Seattle toy store. Not nearly as big as national chain stores, it has the decided advantage over those mega-boxes in that a far smaller percentage of its products are pure junk. You won't find many battery-powered toys, and you'll also be hard pressed to find those heavily advertised toys with pictures of TV or movie characters on them. No *Blue Clues*, *Barbies*, or *Rugrats*: Hooray! Instead, Top Ten features "real" toys that spark the imagination rather than feed their burgeoning consumerist tendencies.

> **Top Ten Toys**
>
> Hours: Sun.-Tues., 9 a.m. - 6 p.m.; Wed.-Fri., 9 a.m. - 9 p.m.
>
> Directions: From I-5 north or south, take the 85th St. exit (#172) and head west. Turn right onto 1st Ave. NW, then turn right into the parking lot.

The math/science and craft areas are particularly well-stocked, as is the "sports" section.

If you're picking up a birthday present on the way to a party, you'll love the do-it-yourself gift-wrapping area right by the door.

Best of all, the staff is knowledgeable, helpful, and playful.

3

South, East and West

The area covered in this chapter is everything south of downtown, West Seattle, Capitol Hill, and Madison Park.

South Seattle

South Seattle is bordered on the north by S Royal Brougham Way and I-90, to the west by the Duwamish Waterway, to the east by Lake Washington, and south by the city limits.

This large geographic chunk of Seattle is comprised of primarily residential areas to the east of I-5 and industrial/warehouse areas to the west. In decades past, there was little of interest to visitors, and some of the areas were considered downright dangerous to someone who was lost.

While this still holds true to a certain extent, my family and I have lived in the south end of Seattle for the past 5 years without regret. For one thing, two of Seattle's greatest negatives are minimized here – traffic and parking. If you stay off I-5 during morning and afternoon commutes, you wouldn't know you were in the city with America's worst traffic problems.

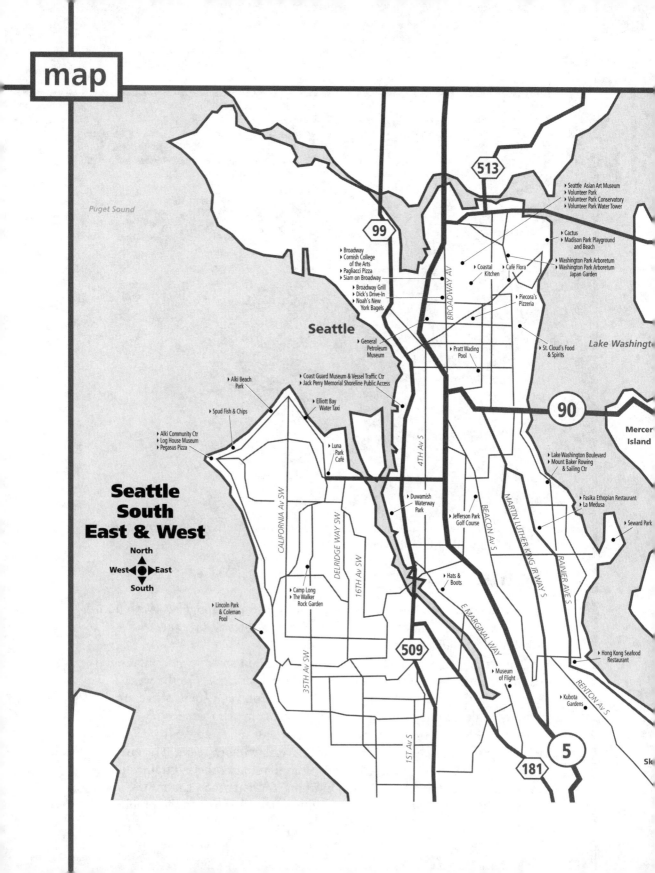

map

Seattle

Seattle South East & West

North
West ◆ East
South

Puget Sound

Lake Washington

Mercer Island

▶ 513
▶ 99
▶ 90
▶ 509
▶ 5
▶ 181

▶ Seattle Asian Art Museum
▶ Volunteer Park
▶ Volunteer Park Conservatory
▶ Volunteer Park Water Tower

▶ Cactus
▶ Madison Park Playground and Beach

▶ Washington Park Arboretum
▶ Washington Park Arboretum Japan Garden

▶ Coastal Kitchen
▶ Café Flora

▶ Piecora's Pizzeria

▶ St. Cloud's Food & Spirits

▶ Broadway
▶ Cornish College of the Arts
▶ Pagliacci Pizza
▶ Siam on Broadway

▶ Broadway Grill
▶ Dick's Drive-In
▶ Noah's New York Bagels

▶ General Petroleum Museum

▶ Pratt Wading Pool

▶ Coast Guard Museum & Vessel Traffic Ctr
▶ Jack Perry Memorial Shoreline Public Access

▶ Alki Beach Park

▶ Elliott Bay Water Taxi

▶ Spud Fish & Chips

▶ Alki Community Ctr
▶ Log House Museum
▶ Pegasus Pizza

▶ Luna Park Café

▶ Lake Washington Boulevard
▶ Mount Baker Rowing & Sailing Ctr

▶ Fasika Ethopian Restaurant
▶ La Medusa

▶ Seward Park

▶ Duwamish Waterway Park

▶ Jefferson Park Golf Course

▶ Lincoln Park & Coleman Pool

▶ Camp Long
▶ The Walker Rock Garden

▶ Hats & Boots

▶ Hong Kong Seafood Restaurant

▶ Museum of Flight

▶ Kubota Gardens

BROADWAY AV

4TH AV S

CALIFORNIA AV SW

DELRIDGE WAY SW

16TH AV SW

35TH AV SW

1ST AV S

BEACON AV S

MARTIN LUTHER KING JR WAY S

RAINIER AV S

E MARGINAL WAY

RENTON AV S

Sk

South, East and West

Southeast Seattle is the nation's most ethnically diverse neighborhood. The most recent census identified some 250 distinct ethnic groups represented here. Everywhere you go, you hear languages other than English being spoken. This is also one of the city's poorest areas, due in no small measure to the large number of recent immigrants who reside here.

Along the shores of Lake Washington, however, you will find some of Seattle's stateliest homes in the neighborhoods of Madrona, Leschi, and Mount Baker, and then there is Seward Park, which many of us consider to be the crown jewel of the city's park system. The best seats for the annual Seafair hydroplane races are here, as are the largest, oldest trees in the city limits.

Lower real estate prices have attracted the young and artistic, who are starting to make such formerly drab places as Columbia City and Georgetown look like good prospects for the hip neighborhoods of the future.

South, East and West

Things to Do

Coast Guard Museum

1519 Alaskan Way (Pier 36)
(206) 217-6993

While not as relevant for the smallest children, it is a must for older kids, especially those with technological or maritime interests.

The museum displays nautical items, ship models, Coast Guard memorabilia, and more than 15,000 photographs dating from the mid-1800s. Other highlights include pieces of wood from the USS *Constitution* and from the rudder of the HMS *Bounty*, lighthouse and buoy lenses, a bell from Admiral Peary's ship, the steam tug *Roosevelt*, old and new uniforms, ships' wheels, and binnacles, among other things.

The real treat here is the Vessel Traffic Center, where the Coast Guard does its job of facilitating the safe and efficient transit of vessel traffic on Puget Sound, much in the same way that the FAA provides air traffic controllers to aviators. The VTS monitors 230,000 vessel movements a year in the 3,500 sq. mi. Puget Sound area. These vessel transits are comprised of mainly large commercial and government craft such as freighters, container ships, tankers, coastal freighters, tugs, fishing vessels, tour boats, Navy ships, and ferries. Older children – and some younger ones – will get a kick out of watching the radar and radio surveillance operators through the viewing window. Free guided tours are available, but as the schedule is variable, you'll need to call first.

**Coast Guard Museum and
Coast Guard Vessel Traffic Center**

Cost: Free

Museum hours:
Mon., Wed., & Fri., 9 a.m. - 3 p.m.;
Sat.-Sun., 1 p.m. - 5 p.m.

Traffic Center hours:
Daily, 8 a.m. - 4 p.m.

Directions: From I-5 north or south, follow signs to "ferries." When you reach Alaskan Way, turn left (instead of right as the signs will direct you). The museum is at Pier 36. Free parking in lot.

South, East and West

Duwamish Waterway Park
Diagonal Ave. S at E Marginal Way (Terminal 108)

For those who grow tired of the rampant gentrification of most of Seattle's more popular neighborhoods, this (along with the Jack Perry Memorial Shoreline Access, see below) is a great place to take your children for a "real" Seattle experience.

Tucked away in a working maritime area, this small park represents the last 2 percent of what once was a massive wetlands and has been set aside by the Port of Seattle as a fish and wildlife habitat. It always amazes us that here amidst the stacks of shipping containers, along a waterway being perpetually plied by working tug boats and other vessels, you will almost always find heron, gulls, geese, and other birds foraging on the muddy shores. Salmon still migrate here with runs of Chinook, chum, pink, sockeye and steelhead, often startling us with powerful leaps and splashes. September is a particularly good time to see salmon.

> **Duwamish Waterway Park**
>
> Directions: From I-5 north or south, follow signs to "ferries." When you reach Alaskan Way, turn left (instead of right as the signs will direct you). Continue south to Diagonal Way S and turn right into the park.

You can walk along the shore, but be prepared for mud. Free parking and picnic tables are available, but there are no bathrooms.

Jack Perry Memorial Shoreline Public Access
Alaskan Way S, south of the Coast Guard Museum

If you spend any time in Seattle, your children will likely become fascinated with the giant red Port of Seattle container cranes that line the mouth of the Duwamish Waterway and the shores of Harbor Island. Seattle's decision to concentrate on container shipping (while rivals, such as Portland, Oregon, stuck with the old pallet shipping methods) is one of the primary reasons the city today stands as the economic engine of the Pacific Northwest.

This is where we like to come to get a first-hand sense of how it all works. You can watch vessels being loaded and unloaded or see the huge container "forklifts" stacking containers as high as office buildings only a few yards away. We're also interested in the small vessels dry-docked here.

South, East and West

Hat & Boots

E Marginal Way at Corson Ave. S

If you're down in this neck of the woods – visiting one of the Duwamish public access parks or visiting the Museum of Flight – this is a fun little drive-by. The giant cowboy hat was once a filling station, while the companion boots served as the lavatories.

Seward Park

5898 Lake Washington Blvd.
www.ci.seattle.wa.us/parks/parkspaces/sewardpark.htm

We think of this as the friendliest park in Seattle. Nearly everyone you meet makes eye contact, smiles, and says, "Hi."

A gem of a park covering nearly 280 acres – 70 of which are shore lands – it is mostly forested with the tallest, oldest trees in the Seattle city limits. Situated on the Bailey Peninsula, which curls out into Lake Washington, Seward Park features a 2 mile paved multi-use (walking, biking, skating) path that never leaves the water's edge. In addition to waterfowl (such as ducks, heron, and coots), we've spotted beaver, turtles, and leaping salmon along the shoreline, not to mention the beautiful water views from every point along the way.

> **Seward Park**
>
> Hours: Daily, 4 a.m. - 11:30 p.m.
>
> Directions: From I-5 north, take the Swift Ave. S/S Albro St. exit (#161). Turn left onto Swift, then right onto S Graham St. Follow Graham to Beacon Ave. S and turn left. Continue on Beacon to S Orcas St. and turn right. Follow Orcas to the entrance of the park. From I-5 south, take the Swift Ave. S/S Albro St. exit (#161) and turn left at the light onto Albro. Cross over the freeway and then turn right onto Swift. Turn left onto S Graham St. and follow directions as above. Free parking in several lots.

Keep an eye out for bald eagles – there are two nesting pairs in this park. (We've often had one or two of these spectacular creatures perched in a tree outside our dining room window, tearing some poor rodent to shreds.)

The unpaved hiking trails that meander through the hilly woods covering the inland part of the park are probably too challenging for children under 4, but a blast for older children who like outdoor adventure. We like to explore with our field guide to Northwest plants so that we can identify the trees and plants we come across.

The charming, grassy amphitheatre (which you can also drive to) is always one of our hiking destinations. Emerging from the woods into its open bowl on the south hillside is like a new discovery each time – it reminds me of something from ancient Greece, and its presence here always strikes me as somehow magical. Josephine likes to mount her own impromptu dancing and singing per- formances for us from the stage. The acoustics are excellent – even in the back

South, East and West

row of benches. Oh yeah, this stage hosts dozens of *other* performances through-out the late spring, summer, and early fall, but not nearly as many as it should.

The playground includes apparatuses that appeal to a variety of ages, but what we like best is that it is a real meeting place for people of all races and nationalities. Josephine plays with children from Africa, the Middle East, Asia, the South Pacific, and Europe, while we grown-ups "use" our children to break down some of the social and cultural barriers that tend to exist between us.

In the summer, the playground atmosphere is carried over to the swimming beach, which is patrolled by lifeguards.

The Seward Park Art Studio is located in a 1927 bathhouse. The studio specializes in pottery and offers a variety of classes for all ages and skill levels. For information, call (206) 722-6342.

Jefferson Park Golf Course

4101 Beacon Ave. S
(206) 762-4513
www.seattlegolf.com

Jefferson Park Golf Course

Greens fees: Adults $25-$28 (18 holes) & $12 (par 3); juniors $10-$13 (18 holes) & $6 (par 3).

Hours: Varies by season; call ahead.

Directions: From I-5 south, take S Columbian Way exit (#163A). Bear right onto S Columbian Way. Turn left onto Beacon Ave. S. Golf course will be on your right. From I-5 north, take Swift/Albro exit (#161). Turn right onto Swift Ave. S. Bear left onto S Eddy St. Turn left onto Beacon Ave. S. Golf course will be on your right. Free parking in lot.

This is the course where PGA champion Fred Couples learned the game. Jefferson Park Golf Course was built in 1917 by the Scotsman Thomas Bendelow, one of America's pioneer golf architects. This public course measures over 6,000 yards and features vistas of the city's skyline and Mt. Rainier. Jefferson Park also includes a nine-hole executive golf course (par 3), restaurant, and practice range.

South, East and West

Museum of Flight

9404 E Marginal Way S
(206) 764-5700 or (206) 764-5720 (24-hour recorded info.)
www.museumofflight.org

"Cool!" That's what children exclaim when stepping into the 6-storey high steel and glass main gallery of this museum, their eyes taking in the dozens of aircraft hanging in formation from the rafters above.

It's impossible to underestimate the influence of Boeing and the aerospace industry on the Puget Sound region, and this is this shrine to it all. Built around the Red Barn that is the birthplace of the Boeing Company, the museum features a magnificent collection of more than 50 flying machines, including a reproduction of Orville and Wilbur Wright's 1902 two-winged glider, an authentic World War I Sopwith Camel, an Apollo Command Module, and the original jumbo jet – the prototype Boeing 747.

The kid's say "cool" again as they sit in the cockpit of a real fighter or tour the first presidential jet.

The staff are knowledgeable; many of them are retired Boeing employees. Tours are free as are the informational films shown in the three on-site theaters. The museum's Wings Café offers a varied menu and a visually exciting, up-close view of neighboring Boeing Field. Call for information about upcoming children's workshops.

It wouldn't be surprising if your visit to the museum inspires a desire to take to the air. If so, Olde Tyme Aviation located adjacent to the back parking lot of the museum might fill the bill. Offering various air tours of the Seattle area (prices ranging from $99-$430) in vintage bi-planes, this is an exciting once-in-a-lifetime adventure. Reservations are not accepted, except in person on the day the ride is desired. Weather, obviously, permitting.

If you just want to watch aircraft take-off and land, Boeing Field (behind the museum) is a place to do it.

Museum of Flight

Cost: Adults $9.50; youths (5-17) $5; children 4 and under are free.

Hours: Daily, 10 a.m.- 5 p.m.; Thurs., open until 9 p.m. Closed Thanksgiving and Christmas Day.

Directions: From I-5 north or south, take exit 158 and head west. Turn right at the first light onto E Marginal Way S. The museum is on the right, and drive 1/2 mile. Free parking.

South, East and West

Mount Baker Rowing and Sailing Center

3800 Lake Washington Blvd. S (Stan Sayres Park)
(206) 386-1913

Mount Baker Rowing and Sailing Center

Directions: From I-5 north or south take exit #163, the Spokane Street/ Columbian Way exit. Choose the Columbian Way lane heading east (do not go west because you will end up on the West Seattle Freeway). As the road turns and heads south, stay in the right lane through two stoplights, then move into the left lane and take the gradual left at the next light (this gets you on Alaskan Way). Continue on this road for about a mile and a half; turn left onto Rainier Avenue South, go two blocks and turn right onto Genesee Street, then go about ten blocks and turn left onto 43rd Avenue South. Lake Washington will be in view at the end of 43rd, and the facility will be to the right, ahead of you. Free parking in lot.

The venue for the 1990 Goodwill Games rowing and sailing competitions and staging area for the annual Seafair hydroplane race, this is a great place for rowing, sailing, kayaking, canoeing, and sail boarding classes for children (13-18) and adults of all ability levels. You may sign up for a class or choose the drop-in option. Call for details.

Every participant must pass a "float test" prior to being permitted on the water. This must be done under the supervision of a lifeguard certified by the American Red Cross. Call for information.

The boat center does not rent boats.

Lake Washington Boulevard

Lake Washington Blvd.

There is nothing more "Seattle" than spending a day enjoying the shores of Lake Washington. From Mt. Baker Beach (just south of the I-90 floating bridge) at the north end to Seward Park at the south, the lakefront is all "public access." Probably the most popular activities during most of the year are walking, jogging, and cycling. During warmer months, there are dozens of places to get your feet wet (including the small lifeguard patrolled Mt. Baker Beach) and to launch small watercraft.

Lake Washington Boulevard

Directions: see directions for Mt. Baker Rowing and Sailing Center.

Although not always acknowledged by motorists, cyclists *always* have the right-of-way along Lake Washington Blvd. From May through September, the road is closed entirely to all but bicycle and pedestrian traffic for what is called "Bicycle Saturdays and Sundays" (usually two weekends per month). For information, call (206) 684-7583 or check the website **www.ci.seattle.wa.us/td/satsun.asp**.

South, East and West

Kubota Gardens

9600 Renton Ave. S (at 55th St. S)
www.ci.seattle.wa.us/parks/parkspaces/Gardens.htm

This is an incredible 20-acre Japanese garden started in 1927 by master landscaper Fujito Kubota, which is now under the care and attention of the city. It's a magical place, full of hidden paths that climb and descend through gorgeously planted hills and valleys. The grounds are interlaced with streams, waterfalls, and ponds in which koi, crayfish, and other creatures lurk. The red lacquered bridges and stepping-stones that cross the waterways are as charming as they are entertaining for little feet. Josephine loves this place.

The spring is the best time to enjoy the flowering trees and shrubs, although summer and fall also have their charms.

Kubota Gardens

Hours: Dawn to dusk.

Directions: From I-5 south, take the Swift/Albro exit (#161). Turn right and cross over the freeway, then turn right onto Swift Ave. S. Follow Swift as it turns east (the street name will change to S Myrtle). Turn right on Martin Luther King Jr. Way S and get immediately into the left lane. Take the slight turn left onto Renton Ave. S and continue to 55th St. S. Kubota Gardens will be on your right. From I-5 north, take exit #158 and head east on S Ryan Way. Turn left on 51st Ave. S. Turn left on Renton Ave. S. Kubota Gardens will be on your left at 55th St. S. Free parking in lot.

Places to Eat

La Medusa

4857 Rainier Ave. S
(206) 723-2192

La Medusa

Hours: Tue.-Thu., 5 p.m. - 9 p.m.
Fri.-Sun., 5 p.m. - 10 p.m.

Directions: From I-5 south, take the S Columbian Way exit (#163A). Keep left at the fork in the ramp and merge onto Columbian Way S. Bear right onto 15th Ave. S. Turn left onto S Columbian Way. Turn right onto S Alaska St. Turn right onto Rainier Ave. S. The restaurant will be on your right. From I-5 north, take the Swift/Albro exit (#161). Turn right onto Swift Ave. S, then left onto S Graham St. Take Graham to Rainier Ave. S and turn left. Continue to Columbia City. Restaurant will be on your left. On-street parking.

This cute Columbia City restaurant has rapidly become an institution in an area that is in the beginning stages of a transformation from nowhere to somewhere. The Italian fare is excellent, although if you don't like raw garlic, make sure you mention it when you order your food. They are willing to whip up special dishes for your kids.

The real draw for Josephine is that young children are given a wad of raw pizza dough to knead as they wait for their food.

South, East and West

Fasika Ethiopian Restaurant

3808 S Edmunds Street
(206) 723-1971

Fasika Ethiopian Restaurant

Hours: Mon.-Thurs., 11 a.m.- 10 p.m.; Fri.-Sat., 11 a.m. - 2 a.m. Fri.-Sat.; Sun., 11 a.m. - 10 p.m.

Directions: From I-5 south, take the S Columbian Way exit (#163A). Keep left at the fork in the ramp and merge onto Columbian Way S. Bear right onto 15th Ave. S. Turn left onto S Columbian Way. Turn right onto S Alaska St. Turn right onto Rainier Ave. S. Turn left onto Edmunds. The restaurant will be on your left. From I-5 north, take the Swift/Albro exit (#161). Turn right onto Swift Ave. S, then left onto S Graham St. Take Graham to Rainier Ave. S and turn left. Continue to Columbia City. Turn right onto Edmunds. Restaurant will be on your left. On-street parking.

This is an extremely casual establishment that almost feels like you've entered a neighborhood hole-in-the-wall in Ethiopia. The authentic food is quite good, albeit a bit oilier than many Americans might like, but since most of the customers seem to be Ethiopian, I doubt they plan to change anything. It might be too exotic for some children, although sopping up the food with the spongy bread is a fun alternative to utensils.

Hong Kong Seafood Restaurant

9400 Rainier Ave. S
(206) 723-1718

A big, bright, simple family place, serving some of the best Chinese food in a city known for its Chinese restaurants. The weekend afternoon dim sum offerings are both delicious and (to this non-Chinese person) sometimes intimidating. Impress your Seattle friends by recommending this relatively unknown place – it's likely they've never been here.

Hong Kong Seafood Restaurant

Direction: From I-5 north or south, take exit # 158 and head east on S Ryan Way. Turn left on 51st Ave. S. Turn right onto Rainier Ave. S. The restaurant will be on your left. Free parking lot.

South, East and West

St. Clouds Food and Spirits

1131 34th Ave.
(206) 726-1522
www.stclouds.com

Named for the orphanage in John Irving's novel "Cider House Rules," this busy neighborhood restaurant boasts a children's menu designed by the owner's son. This includes such delicious, but nutritiously questionable selections as Chocolate Chip Pancakes (breakfast) and Marshmallow Cream and Peanut Butter sandwiches for lunch and dinner. Healthier options, like pasta and quesadillas, are also available. Josephine likes both the food and the enormous selection of toys that are brought to the table as a matter of course.

The adult menu is an eclectic mix of comfort foods (roasted chicken, cheese burgers) and exotica (shrimp ceviche tostadas, chile rubbed New York strip steak with chipotle-honey butter) with entrée prices ranging from $8 to $20.

The service is friendly, fast, and helpful.

St. Clouds Food and Spirits

Hours: Mon., Wed.-Fri., 11 a.m. - 11 p.m.; Sat.-Sun., 9 a.m. - 2 p.m. & 5 p.m. - 11 p.m.; closed Tues.

Directions: From I-5 north, take Madison St. exit and turn right onto Madison. After about a mile, bear right onto E Union St. Go to 34th Ave. E and turn right. From I-5 south, take Union St. exit. Turn left onto 5th Ave., left onto Madison, and follow directions from I-5 north. Free on-street parking.

West Seattle

West of the Duwamish Waterway and north of SW Roxbury St.

West Seattle

Directions: From I-5 north or south take the Spokane St. exit (#163). Follow Spokane onto the West Seattle Freeway across the Duwamish Waterway to West Seattle. Follow directions below to find specific attractions.

On the finger of the peninsula that stretches into Elliott Bay west of Seattle, this neighborhood is the true starting point of the city. The Denny party first landed here at Alki Point in 1851 and only later moved their settlement across the water to what is now Pioneer Square.

The main attractions here are the spectacular skyline views facing east toward downtown and the sandy beaches.

South, East and West

Things to Do

Alki Beach Park

Alki Ave. SW
www.ci.seattle.wa.us/parks/home.htm

Alki Beach Park

Hours: Daily, 4 a.m. - 11 p.m.

Directions: From the West Seattle Freeway, exit onto Harbor Ave. SW (turning right at the light). Continue on Harbor for approximately 2 miles until you've rounded Duwamish Head. Harbor turns into Alki Ave. SW at this point. The park is along the water to your right. Alki Point is some 2 miles farther. Park on-street or in lots, but it can be tight during the summer.

Say "Alki Beach" and most people think of summertime fun in the sand and (always quite cold) surf. And, no doubt, it's a great place for wading, walking, sand castle building, kite flying, volleyball, sunbathing, roller-skating, and leisurely cycling. Get there early on a sunny day, however, as you won't be the only one to have thought of it. In August the beach is the venue for the annual sand castle competition.

Our favorite time to visit Alki Beach is during an ultra-low tide, in whatever season it takes place. When the tide falls back, it reveals acres upon acres of tide pools, seething with incredible Northwest sea life – starfish, shellfish of all kinds, crabs, anemones, sea slugs, you name it. Turn over a few rocks to see what scuttles out from beneath it. Just don't take things home with you! Come prepared to get muddy and wet and don't forget your rubber boots. You might also bring a thermos of something hot for afterwards.

Alki Point Lighthouse and Coast Guard Station (3201 Alki Ave. SW) features a circular staircase that children enjoy climbing. The Coast Guard provides free tours on weekends and holidays. Call (206) 286-5423 for information.

Roller blading at Alki Beach park with Elliot Bay in foreground, Seattle skyline in background

courtesy Nick Gunderson

South, East and West

Camp Long

5200 35th Ave. SW
(206) 684-7434
www.ci.seattle.wa.us/parks/home.htm

Camp Long

Directions: The West Seattle Freeway ends at a traffic light at 35th Ave. SW. Turn left on 35th Avenue SW. Go eight-tenths of a mile to Dawson St. Take a left on Dawson and you will enter the park. Free parking in lot.

This 68-acre nature preserve is one of those places that locals (outside of West Seattle) know little about. Our friend Tevan's father (a long-time Seattle resident) recently returned from a hike, enthusiastic over the concept that "You can camp there overnight! Right inside the city limits!" By "camping" he meant that one can rent one of the 10 rustic cabins equipped with double bunk beds (sleeping accommodations for 12), electric lights, table, stone fireplace, and running water outside each cabin. Cabins are $35 per night (plus a refundable $50 damage deposit) with a 2-night maximum. This is an excellent way to introduce city kids to the idea of

courtesy Seattle Parks & Recreation

Camp Long Lodge

camping – and if it doesn't work out, at least you're only minutes away from civilization in the form of beds with sheets, central heating, and television. Call for reservations.

The "Fire Ring" is an uncovered campfire circle, with log benches to accommodate up to 100. Reservations and deposit required.

The nation's first manmade climbing rock is here, as well as an artificial "glacier" – sometimes it's free (call for schedule), but usually there is a small fee required. Climbing classes are available for children 7+, as is an extensive schedule of nature programs for all ages and interests.

Hiking, either on your own or under the guidance of a naturalist (call for a tour reservation), is a popular activity. You're not going to want to take a stroller, so know your child's limits.

South, East and West

Lincoln Park and Coleman Pool

8011 Fauntleroy SW (at SW Webster)
www.ci.seattle.wa.us/parks/home.htm
(206) 684-7494

For those seeking a more urban outdoor experience in West Seattle than Camp Long (see above), Lincoln Park is a 130-acre beauty.

Crisscrossed by paved walking/biking trails, the "forest" is civilized and the views of the Olympic Mountains (on a clear day) from the bluff or rocky beach are unsurpassed. The tide pools are a fun low-tide activity and the two playgrounds are up to snuff (one was renovated in 1998). Also includes playfields, tennis and horseshoe courts, picnic shelters, and restrooms.

Up until the 1940s, there was a real salt-water swimming hole here, fed by the Puget Sound waters. This has been replaced by Coleman Pool, which still features salt water, now, thankfully, of the heated variety. Only open during summer months, this pool rivals Magnolia's "Pop" Mounger Pool (see North Seattle) in our affections. There is also a wading pool. Call for schedule.

courtesy Seattle Parks & Recreation

Coleman Pool

Alki Community Center

5817 SW Stevens St.
(206) 684-7430
www.ci.seattle.wa.us/parks/Centers/index.htm

As with the other 24 community centers operated by Seattle Parks and Recreation, Alki offers a wide array of programs and special events for families, including after school care, piano and ballet classes, day camps, and other programs. Ping-pong, billiards, and basketball are available on a drop-in basis, and your children will love the newly renovated playground.

Annual events include a spring egg hunt, community picnics, a salmon barbecue, and a Halloween Carnival. Call for specifics.

Probably the most popular activity is Friday night roller-skating in the gym from September through May, which draws some 100 participants each week. You can bring your own skates or rent them.

South, East and West

Log House Museum

3003 62nd Ave. SW
(206) 938-5293

We're not suggesting you go out of your way to visit this little museum, but if you or your child has a particular interest in Seattle's history – or if you just need a break from the beach, which is just a block away – this place commemorates the landing of the Denny party in 1851. An interesting, quaint collection of memorabilia.

Log House Museum

Cost: Free

Hours: Tues., Noon - 7 p.m.;
Fri.-Sat., 10 a.m.- 4 p.m.;
Sun., Noon - 3 p.m.

Directions: From the West Seattle Freeway, exit onto Harbor Ave. SW (turning right at the light). Continue on Harbor for approximately 2 miles until you've rounded Duwamish Head. Harbor turns into Alki Ave. SW at this point. Turn left onto 61st Ave. SW and continue one block to SW Stevens St. Museum is on the corner.

Elliott Bay Water Taxi

Seacrest Park (1660 Harbor Ave. SW)
(206) 553-3000
www.transit.metrokc.gov/bus/bulletins/water_taxi.html

Elliott Bay Water Taxi

Hours: Mon.-Thurs., 6:45 a.m. - 7 p.m.;
Fri, 6:45 a.m. - 10:30 p.m.;
Sat-Sun., 8:30 a.m. - 10:30 p.m.

Cost: $2; under 5 ride for free.

The cheapest way to get out on the water. Although its primary function is to ferry commuters, we like taking the round-trip just for fun. Many West Seattle residents hop the "taxi," which lands at Pier 54 on the waterfront, for quick, stress-free visits to downtown and Pike Place Market.

The Walker Rock Garden

5407 37th Ave. SW
(206) 935-3036

An honest to goodness labor of love, the Walker Rock Garden is unlike anything you'll ever see anywhere else. It's a wonderland of petrified wood, agates, colored glass, semi-precious stones, shells, and just plain old rocks Milton Walker built in the yard of his house over the course of 30 years. You will find walls and towers, benches, lakes, an "airport," and many other magical monuments and sculptures. It's truly impossible to put the charm of this place into words. It's a real fantasyland, unlike anything you have ever seen.

The Walker family still lives in the house, so you must call and make an appointment several days in advance.

The Walker Rock Garden

Cost: Free, although donations are welcome.

Hours: By appointment.

Directions: Take West Seattle Freeway until it ends, continue to 37th Ave. SW and turn left. Park on the street. (The rock garden is not visible from the street.)

South, East and West

Places to Eat

Spud Fish & Chips

2666 Alki Ave. SW (about at the halfway point of Alki Beach Park)
(206) 938-0606

Spud Fish & Chips

Hours: Daily,
11 a.m. - 9 p.m.

This is the original Spud Fish & Chips (the other Seattle location is near Green Lake). A regular contender for the best fish and chips in this city of fish and chips, Spud is better for take-out (across the street is Alki Beach Park) than eating in. We like the basic cod the best, although halibut, prawns, clams, and oysters are also available. This food is delivered to your hands HOT enough to burn an adult's tongue, let alone a small child's – let it cool before sinking your teeth into the toothsome corn meal crust.

Pegasus Pizza

2758 Alki Ave. SW (about at the halfway point of Alki Beach Park)
(206) 932-4849

Pegasus Pizza

Hours: Daily,
Noon - 11 p.m.

Across the street from Alki Beach Park, Pegasus features one of Seattle's favorite pizzas, the crust being the thing most people rave about. The notorious "Greek" pizza includes feta, olives, mushrooms, green peppers, and all those other things that Josephine thinks ruin an otherwise perfectly good slice. Fortunately, they have great cheese pizza as well.

Nice views, a cheerful wait staff, and a take-out option for those eager to get back to the beach. You might find yourself standing on line during peak hours in the summer.

Luna Park Café

2918 SW Avalon Way
(206) 935-7250

Luna Park Café

Hours: Daily, 7 a.m. - 11 p.m.

Directions: From the West Seattle Freeway, exit onto Harbor Ave. SW. Turn left at the light onto 30th Ave. SW. The street name will change to Avalon. The café will be on your right.

This place is a real 1950s soda fountain with a retro décor sure to delight the kids. Jukeboxes, pinball games, and all kinds of other memorabilia line the walls and shelves. The menu isn't fancy, the prices cheap, and the portions huge.

South, East and West

Capitol Hill, Madison Park, and Points in Between

These neighborhoods in east-central Seattle are as far apart demographically as they are close together geographically.

Capitol Hill is a diverse, hip, urban neighborhood where pierced, tattooed street youths mingle with retired pensioners, panhandlers, and earnest college students stooped under gigantic backpacks. It's a vibrant, strange, beautiful, and grungy place, especially along Broadway.

Directly east from Capitol Hill, along the shores of Lake Washington lies the affluent neighborhood of Madison Park, with its shady, tree-lined streets, large, expensive homes, and pricey tennis club.

Capitol Hill, Madison Park, and Points in Between

Directions to Capitol Hill: From I-5 south, take the Deny Way exit (#166). Turn left on Denny Way and cross back over the freeway. Turn left on Olive Way and continue to Broadway. From I-5 north, take the Olive Way exit (#166). Continue on Olive to Broadway. On-street metered parking.

Directions to Madison Park: From I-5 south, take Union Street exit (#165B). Turn left on 6th Ave. and continue to Madison St. Turn left on Madison and follow it for about 2.5 miles. Once you've crossed McGilvra Blvd., you are in the Madison Park retail area. From I-5 north, take the Madison St. exit (#165). Turn right on Madison St. and follow directions as above. Free on-street parking.

Things to Do

Walk along Broadway

If you're not put-off by "alternative" lifestyles, there is really nothing more entertaining than simply taking a walk on Broadway on a sunny afternoon. Your child will love the swirl of creative "costumes," bizarre hairstyles, and make-up on steroids. When Josephine asks me why people are dressed this way, I tell her, "Because they want people to look at them," which I think is mostly true.

On a nice day, you'll enjoy street performers playing jazz, traditional Irish, or funky folk music. Between E Republican and Howell St., you will find the bronze footprints of artist Jack Mackie's "Dancer's Series." I've never met a child who didn't want to stop and try to perform these ballroom dances.

South, East and West

Cornish College of the Arts

710 E Roy St.
(206) 726-5066 (events hotline)
(206) 726-5016 (admissions)
www.cornish.edu

Dance, music, and theater are performed by both students and professional artists. In particular, performances by the Junior Dance Company will be of interest to your children. Our friend Alicia loves her ballet classes at Cornish.

Cornish College of the Arts

Directions: Follow Broadway north to E Roy St. Turn left and continue one block. The college is on your right.

Volunteer Park

1247 15th Ave. E
www.cityofseattle.net/parks

Volunteer Park

Directions: Cross Broadway on Olive (it becomes John St.; heading east). Continue to 15th Ave. E. Turn left and proceed about a mile to E Prospect St. and turn left. The entrance to free parking lot is on the right.

This nearly 50-acre park has a lot to offer families: the Seattle Asian Art Museum (see below), the Volunteer Park Conservatory (see below), wading pool, playground, and lots of paths and trails to explore.

This is our favorite hot day playground (located in the northeast corner of the park) because it is mostly shaded and the metal slides don't get too hot to touch. The wading pool is filled each day (around 11 a.m.) during summer months, with fresh, chlorinated water. This is a very popular place for day-campers during the summer, and the "big kids'" rowdy play can intimidate some younger children. No lifeguards.

The bathrooms are not terribly close to the playground/pool and are sometimes disgusting. Avoid the park after dark.

Volunteer Park Conservatory

North side of Volunteer Park (see above for directions)
www.cityofseattle.net/parks/parkspaces/conservatory.htm

Volunteer Park Conservatory

Cost: Free

Hours: Daily, 10 a.m. - 7 p.m., including holidays.

Divided into "five houses" with a variety of climates, the conservatory – opened in 1912 – is a wonderland containing thousands of species from climates warmer than that of the Northwest. The Bromeliad House contains some 2,000 members of the pineapple family with their colorful leaves and flowers. The Fern House includes a rotating display of plants around a small pond – check out the carnivorous plants along its boggy shore. The Palm House is home to a spectacular display of orchids, and the Seasonal Display House features plants from temperate climates. The air in the Cactus House is noticeably drier – the Jade Plant is nearly 100 years old and blooms in November and January.

South, East and West

Seattle Asian Art Museum

Volunteer Park (see above for directions)
(206) 654-3100
www.seattleartmuseum.org

A division of the Seattle Art Museum, the permanent collection here focuses on Chinese and Japanese art and culture. Special exhibits tend to concentrate on other Asian cultures. Smaller children will be bored, but older kids – especially those who are prepared with a bit of knowledge about Asian cultures – will get a lot out of a visit.

> **Seattle Asian Art Museum**
>
> General admission tickets: Adults $7, students/seniors $5, children under 12 free when accompanied by adult. First Thurs. of each month admission to permanent exhibits is free.
>
> Hours: Wed.-Sun., 10 a.m. - 5 p.m.; Thurs., 10 a.m. - 9 p.m. Closed Columbus Day, Thanksgiving, Christmas Eve and Day, and New Year's Eve and Day.

Volunteer Park Water Tower

Northside of Volunteer Park

For those with energy to burn, the climb up the 106 steps to the observation deck of this 75-foot tower is a challenge. The views from the top are worthwhile, but avoid the tower after dark.

> **Volunteer Park Water Tower**
>
> Cost: Free
>
> Hours: Daily, 8 a.m. - 5:30 p.m.

Washington Park Arboretum

Lake Washington Blvd. between 40th Ave. E and E Madison on the south, to the 520 Bridge and Lake Washington on the north.
Visitor's Center: 2300 Arboretum Dr. E
(206) 543-8800 (Visitor's Center)
(206) 325-4510 (Arboretum Foundation Office)
www.depts.washington.edu/wpa

courtesy Washington Park Arboretum

This 200-acre park is one of Seattle's greatest treasures, with walking trails meandering amongst some 40,000 trees, shrubs, and vines representing 4,600 different species, including 139 plants on the endangered species list. Collections include rhododendrons, azaleas, mountain ash, pine, spruce, cedar, fir, crabapple, holly, magnolia, camellia, and Japanese maple.

The Arboretum offers a variety of educational programs throughout the year for children and adults. Call (206) 543-8801 for details.

South, East and West

Springtime, with the shrubs and trees in bloom, is the most spectacular time to visit, although some prefer the fall colors.

Drop by or call the Visitor's Center for tips on which sections will be the most interesting during your visit – each season offers something special. You can take a self-guided tour by grabbing a brochure or hook up with one of the weekend, guided tours (not recommended for small children who are unable to walk for 1-2 hours).

Arboretum Guided Tour

courtesy Washington Park Arboretum

Popular with photographers, artists, and joggers, the Waterfront Trail is one of our favorite Arboretum walks. This 1/2 mile trail begins on Foster Island (the trailhead is about 1/2 mile north of the visitor's center) and takes you through the largest wetland in Seattle. You cross floating bridges to Marsh Island and again to the mainland where you will find the Museum of History and Industry (see North Seattle) and the Montlake Cut. There are several observation outposts offering views of Lake Washington and wetland areas. Waterfowl abound, as do frogs, turtles, and other creatures. In the summer, water lilies are abundantly in bloom. Of particular interest is how this natural habitat co-exists with urban development, such as Highway 520, which was built right over the wetlands. Some parts of the floating bridges are without railings, so you'll want to hold hands. A heavy-duty stroller pushed by a fit adult could navigate the trail, but it would be a workout. As with the other Arboretum trails, boots are recommended during the fall, winter, and early spring. A self-guided Waterfront Trail brochure is available at the visitor's center.

The Arboretum offers a variety of educational programs throughout the year for children and adults. Call (206) 543-8801 for details.

The Arboretum Foundation holds plant sales each Tuesday throughout the year from 10 a.m. - noon at the Pat Calvert Greenhouse. Arboretum members donate plants from their own gardens for sale on Wednesdays, March-October, 10 a.m. - 2 p.m. and every 2nd Saturday, April-September, 10 a.m. - 2 p.m. Special spring and fall sales are also held. Call for details.

The Arboretum's Japanese Garden requires a separate admission (see below).

Washington Park Arboretum

Cost: Free

Hours: Grounds and trails open daily, 7 a.m. - dusk. Visitor's Center open daily, 10 a.m. - 4 p.m.

Directions: From Madison Park, drive west on Madison St. to Lake Washington Blvd. E; turn right into the Arboretum. From I-5 north or south, take exit 168 (Bellevue-Kirkland) onto Hwy. 520; take first exit to Lake Washington Blvd. E, and follow it into the Arboretum. From east of Lake Washington: drive east on the Evergreen Point Bridge (Hwy. 520) to the first Seattle exit (Lake Washington Blvd. S); from the ramp turn left into the Arboretum. Free parking lots.

South, East and West

Washington Park Arboretum Japanese Garden

Lake Washington Blvd., 2 blocks north of Madison St.
(206) 684-4725

One of the most highly acclaimed Japanese Gardens outside of Japan, this park is beautiful from March through September, but particularly so during the spring when most of the plants are in bloom. If you can keep your children on the paths, they will have fun. The large koi (think giant goldfish) pond is a winner. We've been invited to help feed the fish when visiting during feeding time (afternoons).

Tea ceremonies are performed spring through fall, although the teahouse itself is for viewing only. Call for schedule.

Tours may be arranged for large groups, as well as families or children. Tours cover the culture, philosophy, and horticulture of the garden, tailored for the specific tour participants. Please make tour arrangements two weeks in advance.

> **Washington Park Arboretum Japanese Garden**
>
> Cost: Adults $2.50, children 6-18 $1.50, under 6 free.
>
> Season/Hours: Mar. 1-Sep. 9. Daily, 10 a.m.- dusk, including holidays.

Madison Park Playground and Beach

E Madison St. & E Howe St. (on Lake Washington)
www.cityofseattle.net/parks

> **Madison Park Playground and Beach**
>
> Directions: Continue on E Madison St. all the way to Lake Washington. The beach is right in front of you.

We often make a day of Madison Park with this playground and beach as the centerpiece. Getting acquainted with new kids is easy here, whilst enjoying the huge sandbox, slides, swings, and climb structure. There is one tall, wooden structure obviously left over from a time before safety regulations (e.g., there is a railing around the 7-foot high platform, but the vertical supports must be a foot apart). Naturally, this is Josephine's favorite piece of equipment.

Across the street, you'll find the grass and sand beach where lifeguards patrol during the summer. This is a great place for watching the Blue Angel aerial performances if you happen to be here in August during Seafair. The bathrooms are pretty good as far as public beach facilities go.

South, East and West

General Petroleum Museum

1526 Bellevue Ave.
(206) 323-4789

General Petroleum Museum

Hours: Tues.-Sat., by appointment.

Directions: Take Broadway south (past Seattle Central Community College), turn right on Pine St. and follow it until it intersects with Bellevue Ave. (about 1/4 mile). The museum is upstairs at the intersection.

For years, I would pass this museum, see the red neon winged horse of the Mobil Oil sign aglow in the window and think, "How can anyone live with that thing in their living room?" It wasn't until I attended a party here that I discovered the true nature of the place: a nostalgic shrine to all things oil-related. With some 15,000 items on display at any given time, this labor of love includes vintage gas pumps, signage, advertisements, and other petroleum-based artifacts from as far back as 1890 and ranging right up to about the time of the energy crisis in the 1970s.

Pratt Wading Pool

1800 S Main St.
(206) 684-7796

This is actually not a wading pool, but rather the most elaborate garden sprinkler you've ever seen. Water spouts from the continent of Africa on the ground as well as from the water cannons that are shaped like safari animals. It's a fun place, but kids can't help running on the wet surface, often with the catastrophic results you warned them about.

Pratt Wading Pool

Hours: Late spring through summer.

Directions: From I-5 north, take Madison St. exit (#165) and turn right onto Madison. Turn right on Boren Ave. Turn left on E Yesler Way. Turn right on 20th Ave. Pool will be on your right at Main St. From I-5 south, take Union St. exit (#165B) and turn left on 5th. Turn left on Madison and follow directions as above.

South, East and West

Places to Eat

Pagliacci Pizza

426 Broadway E
(206) 324-0730

This locally-owned chain of pizzerias is regularly recognized as Seattle's favorite pizza. Broadway is a great people watching area, and the window seats here are some of the best spots in town for partaking in this activity.

> **Pagliacci Pizza**
>
> Hours: Sun-Thu 11 a.m.-11 p.m.; Fri-Sat 11 a.m. -12 a.m.
>
> Directions: Follow directions to Capitol Hill. Turn left onto Broadway and drive about 2 1/2 blocks. Restaurant is on the right.

Broadway Grill

314 Broadway Ave. E
(206) 328-7000

Popular, noisy, with average food, this is the place for a family that can't agree on a particular type of food. The grill, fryer food, pastas, and children's menu are up to snuff, while the more elaborate and exotic entrees are uneven at best. We stick with the basics and – when it's just the two of us – choose to sit at the counter to watch the cooks in the open kitchen. Your boy will get a kick out of using the (usually) ice-filled urinal.

Adults can get real drinks here.

> **Broadway Grill**
>
> Hours: Mon-Fri., 9 a.m. - 2 a.m.; Sat.-Sun., 8 a.m. - 2 a.m.
>
> Directions: Follow directions to Capitol Hill. Turn left on Broadway and drive 1 1/2 blocks. Restaurant is on the right.

Siam on Broadway

616 Broadway E
(206) 324-0892

My wife, Jennifer, and I have been eating here since well before there was a Thai restaurant across the street from every Starbucks in Seattle. Josephine doesn't care for the traditionally spicy Thai cuisine (in fact, the last time we ate here, we smuggled in a slice of Pagliacci cheese pizza), but the kitchen will prepare plain noodles, rice and big, yummy spring rolls. The open kitchen is probably smaller than the one you have at home – there is high entertainment value in sitting at the counter to watch the four-woman kitchen staff perform their little culinary ballet in this tight space. The fish tank can also bemuse antsy tots.

> **Siam on Broadway**
>
> Hours: Mon.-Thurs., 11:30 a.m. - 10 p.m.; Fri., 11:30 a.m. - 11 p.m.; Sat., 5 p.m. - 11 p.m.; Sun., 5 p.m. - 10 p.m.
>
> Directions: Follow directions to Capitol Hill. Turn left on Broadway and drive 4 1/2 blocks. Restaurant is on the right.

In most Thai restaurants, we request our food "medium" spicy, but here we've found we need to ask for "mild."

South, East and West

Coastal Kitchen

429 15th Ave. E
(206) 322-1145

Coastal Kitchen

Hours: Mon.-Fri., 8:30 a.m. - Midnight;
Sat.-Sun, 8:30 a.m. - 3 p.m. & 5 p.m. - Midnight.

Directions: Follow directions to Capitol Hill. Continue across Broadway on E. John St. and proceed to 15th Ave. E. Turn left and drive about 2 1/2 blocks. Restaurant is on the left.

"Coastal" refers to this restaurant's theme of serving food from "coasts" around the world. Depending upon when you dine, you'll be offered Cajun, Thai, Mediterranean, or just about anything from anywhere with access to water. The surprise is that they do it well – often spectacularly. The regular menu, likewise, and breakfast are served all day. The children's menu is extensive, featuring all of the things typically associated with the pre-adolescent palate.

We have had slow service here on busy nights, so come prepared with coloring books.

Dick's Drive-In

115 Broadway E
(206) 323-1300

Dick's Drive-In

Hours: Daily, 10:30 a.m. - 2 a.m.

Directions: Follow directions to Capitol Hill. Turn left on Broadway and drive 1/2 block. Restaurant is on the right.

I've included Dick's in this guide because it's a local institution, and when you see the people lining up, you'll wonder what you're missing – burgers, fries, shakes. If you want food quick and to go, it's a notch up from McDonald's. Its popularity has a great deal to do with nostalgia.

Cactus

4220 E Madison St.
(206) 324-4140

Great Mexican and Southwestern basics, but it's the lesser-known dishes that keep the crowds coming in. Josephine feeds greedily on the cheese quesadilla and fantastic fresh homemade chips and salsa. I generally order whatever they're serving with their mole sauce. We like the brightly painted tables and chili pepper bedecked rafters.

Cactus

Hours: Mon.-Sat., 11:30 a.m. - 3 p.m. & 5 - 10:30 p.m.; Sun., 5 p.m. - 10 p.m.

Directions: See directions to Madison Park.

Reservations are not accepted. Our strategy is to show up early (5:30 - 6 p.m.) and we've never had trouble getting a seat.

South, East and West

Café Flora

2901 E Madison Street
(206) 325-9100
www.cafeflora.com

This vegetarian institution in Madison Valley is popular with families for weekend brunch, lunch, and early dinner. They work hard here to create exotic, exciting vegetarian dishes and succeed more often than not. If given a choice, take a seat in the beautiful atrium. Save room for dessert.

Café Flora

Hours: Tues.-Fri., 11:30 a.m. - 10 p.m.; Sat., 9 a.m. - 2 p.m. & 5 p.m. - 10 p.m.; Sun., 9 a.m. - 2 p.m.; closed Mon.

Directions: See directions to Washington Park Arboretum. The restaurant is on the south side of the street near the entrance to the arboretum.

Noah's New York Bagels

220 Broadway East
(206) 720-2925
www.noahs.com

Jennifer insists that this is the only "good, New York style" bagel bakery in town. Josephine likes hers with a shmeer of "pink" (strawberry) cream cheese. Noah's also prepares excellent party trays.

Noah's New York Bagels

Hours: Daily, 7 a.m.- 7 p.m.

Directions: Follow directions to Capitol Hill. Turn left on Broadway and drive 1/2 block. Restaurant is on the right.

Piecora's Pizzeria

1401 E Madison St.
(206) 322-9411

Not really near anything else in this book, Piecora's is, for us, a destination pizza joint, serving the best pies in Seattle. I'm so confident of the quality of their product that I even recommend it to New Yorkers! It's something of a dive, the staff can be sullen, and the music too loud, but if you just *need* New York style thin-crust pizza, come here. If you've dragged someone with you who doesn't eat pizza, steer them toward one of the gigantic salads. Take out is a popular option.

Piecora's Pizzeria

Hours: Mon.-Thurs., 11:30 a.m. - 11 p.m.; Fri.-Sat., 11:30 a.m. - 12 a.m.; Sun., 12 p.m. - 10 p.m.

Directions: From I-5 north, take Madison St. exit (#165). Turn right onto Madison and continue east to 14th Ave. Piecora's is on the southeast corner of the intersection. Turn right on 14th, then immediately left (can be a tough turn) into the parking lot behind the pizzeria. From I-5 south, take Union exit (#165B). Turn left on 5th Ave. Proceed to Madison St. and turn left. Proceed as per directions from I-5 north.

4

Beyond The City Limits

The Eastside

The Eastside refers to everything east of Lake Washington all the way into the foothills of the Cascade Mountains. This includes the cities of Bellevue, Kirkland, Redmond, Issaquah (say: "Issa Kwah"), and dozens of other towns and communities.

Puget Sound

5

Everett Aquasox
(Everett Memorial Stadium)

Everett

Snohomish

9

Boeing
Factory
Tour

101

104

99

104

Edmonds City Park
Old Milltown

Edmonds

513

Kirkland public art
& downtown
(Marina Park)

203

2

Boehm's Chocolates
Marine Science Ctr
Poulsbo
Sluys Bakery

522

Skykomish

Bloedel
Reserve

Winslow
Bainbridge Island
Steamliner Diner
Waterfront Park

Kirkland

520

Skate King

Remlinger Farms

Bainbridge
Island

Bellevue

202

Bellevue Botanical Garden
Kelsey Creek
Park/Farm

Denny Creek Trail

Fall City

3

Bremerton
Bremerton Naval
Museum
USS Turner Joy
(Bremerton Waterfront)

Bremerton

Seattle

405

Snoqualmie Falls

Snoqualmie

Port Orchard

Winghaven Park

900

Bellevue Square
Mercer Slough Nature Park
Rosalie Whyel Museum
of Doll Art

Renton

90

Snoqualmie
Pass

16

Fox
Island

3

509

18

Paradise
Ridge
Park

Vashon

Vashon
Island

99

169

Skiing
(Summit at Snoqualmie)

Burton Acres-Jensen Point Park
Burton Adventure Recreation Ctr

Fort Nisqually Historic Site
Never Never Land Family
Picnic Playground
Point Defiance Park Zoo
& Aquarium

Tacoma

Squaxin
Island

Gig Harbor

Children's Museum
of Tacoma
Tacoma Rainiers
Tacoma Nature
Center

**Seattle
Area**

101

161

North

3

West

East

South

12

Olympia

5

7

Northwest Trek

**MOUNT
RAINIER**

Beyond The City Limits

Things to Do

Bellevue Square

NE 8th and Bellevue Way NE
Bellevue
(425) 454-8096
www.bellevuesquare.com

Bellevue Square

Hours: Mon.-Sat., 9:30 a.m. - 9:30 p.m;
Sun., 11 a.m. - 7 p.m.

Directions: From I-5 north or south, take
I-90 exit (toward "Spokane"). Cross the
lake and take the Bellevue Way exit.
Follow Bellevue Way to NE 8th. Free
parking in mall garages/lots.

Again, breaking our rule of *not* including shopping malls in this book, "Bell Square" is really the heart of the state's 5th largest city. A well-managed, relatively upscale indoor shopping mall, you will find most of the area's major department stores, national chains, and a decent selection of smaller retailers. The main attractions for the kids (aside from retailers like FAO Schwartz and The Disney Store) are the two well-padded play boats, which are nearly always crowded with children, moms, and nannies. The upstairs boat – designed to look like a Washington State Ferry – is usually less busy and therefore more appropriate for smaller children.

You can rent strollers.

Kelsey Creek Park/Farm

13204 SE 8th Pl.
Bellevue
(425) 455-7688
www.ci.bellevue.wa.us/Parks/majorparks/kelsey.htm

Kelsey Creek Park/Farm

Directions: From I-5 north or south, take
the I-90 exit. Cross the lake, then take
the I-405 exit heading north (toward
Everett). Take the SE 8th St. exit and
head east. Pass under the train trestle
and go straight across the Lake Hills
Connector Road. The road will wind
through a residential area, continue
straight after the first stop sign. Where
the street comes to a "T" (at the second
stop sign), turn left, and the park will
be on the right. Signs give directions to
the parking lot.

There are hiking trails, a nice playground and a picnic area, but the main attraction is the farm where you will find bunnies, horses, chickens, cows, goats, sheep, pigs, and other barnyard denizens, all available for up-close viewing, and some for touching. There is a big red barn and white fences – very attractive. Spring is when the babies are born.

Beyond The City Limits

Bellevue Botanical Garden

12001 Main St.
Bellevue
(425) 451-3755

Bellevue Botanical Garden

Directions: From I-5 north or south, take the I-90 exit, cross the lake, then take I-405 heading north (toward Everett). Take the NE 8th St. exit, heading east. Turn right on 124th Ave. NE. Park is on your left.

This garden is actually several gardens featuring a variety of plant-types, including rhododendrons, ground covers, perennials, and others. Josephine likes the water features, such as the fountain by the visitor's center and the new "waterfall" that cascades over many levels and under several naturalistic bridges. The Yao Garden (Japanese) is also a favorite, with its paths and shrines.

Obviously, the spring and summer are the best times to visit for blossoms, but we prefer December when holiday lights are fashioned into a garden of winter blooms. Magic!

Rosalie Whyel Museum of Doll Art

1116 108th Ave. NE
Bellevue
(425) 455-1116
www.halcyon.com/dollart

Rosalie Whyel Museum of Doll Art

Cost: Adults $6, children 5-17 $4, 4 and under are free.

Hours: Mon.-Sat., 10 a.m. - 5 p.m.; Sun., 1 p.m. - 5 p.m.

Directions: From I-5 north or south, take the I-90 exit (toward Spokane), cross the lake, and take the I-405 exit heading north (toward Everett). Take the NE 8th exit (westbound). Turn right on 108th Ave. NE. The museum is a peach-colored mansion at the intersection with NE 12th St.

With more than 3,000 dolls on display, this is a must-see for doll lovers of all ages. The museum is home to dolls from all over the world (some as much as 150 years old), dollhouses, clothing and everything else "dolly," including the very first Barbie. The museum store sells antique and modern collectables.

Mercer Slough Nature Park

2102 Bellevue Way SE
Bellevue
(425) 452-2752

Mercer Slough Nature Park

Directions: From I-5 north or south, take I-90 exit (toward Spokane), cross the lake, and take the Bellevue Way exit. The slough is to your right. Free parking at the Sweyolocken Boat Launch (3000 Bellevue Way SE), the Blueberry Farm (2380 Bellevue Way SE), or the Winters House (2102 Bellevue Way SE).

A 5-mile, easy hiking trail takes you through this 320-acre nature preserve, which is Lake Washington's largest remaining wetland. Hundreds of plant species and over 170 wildlife species live here, including coyote (it is a bizarre experience to come into face-to-face contact with one of these creatures), beaver, and muskrat. The trails – a system of elevated boardwalks and dirt and paved trails – can be awfully muddy during late fall, winter, and early spring, so bring boots.

A secondary paved trail for bicycles and skates encircles the park.

Beyond The City Limits

On the east side of the park, you will find the Environmental Education Center, which provides educational programs and guided canoe tours. Call for information and schedules. Bathrooms are available at the Blueberry Farm and the Winters House, as well as the Education Center.

Kirkland Public Art and Downtown

Start at Marina Park
Kirkland

Kirkland Public Art and Downtown

Directions: From I-5, take either I-90 or State Route 520 over Lake Washington, then exit onto I-405 heading north. Take exit #18 and head west on Central Way NE. Marina Park is at the end of Central on the lake. Free lot and street parking available, although sometimes difficult during summer months.

More than a dozen bronze, aluminum, and stone sculptures sprout from the streets of downtown Kirkland, many portray children, and all will delight real kids. Grab a map from the special display stand near the park or from a local merchant and take yourself on a self-guided tour of the artworks. Kirkland's downtown and waterfront is a pleasant, entertaining place to spend some time, and the search for statues is a fun way to do it.

"Puddle Jumpers," located in Marina Park itself, featuring a gang of six children leaping into the mud, is one of our favorites, as is "Leap Frog," located in Marsh Park.

Kirkland's many art galleries band together to host an ArtWalk from 6 - 9 p.m. on the second Thursday of each month, year-round.

You will find dozens of restaurants as you explore, most of which cater to families.

Remlinger Farms

32610 NE 32nd St.
Carnation
(425) 333-4135
www.rfarm.com

Remlinger Farms

Cost: $5 (more for special events).

Season/Hours: Season Opening – Mother's Day Weekend; Spring Hours (May/June) – Open Sat. and Sun. only, 11 a.m. - 5 p.m.; Summer Hours (July/August) – Daily, 11 a.m. - 5 p.m.; Fall Hours (September) – Open Sat. and Sun. only, 11 a.m. - 5 p.m.

Directions: From I-5 north or south, take I-90 exit (toward Spokane) and continue past Issaquah to the Preston-Fall City exit (#22). Follow signs to Fall City. In Fall City, at the stop sign, go straight over the bridge. After the bridge, make an immediate left onto highway #203 north for 5 miles. At the Remlinger Farms sign, turn right onto NE 32nd St. and go 1/4 mile.

We love coming here in October for the annual "Fall Harvest Festival," which is also when everyone else in the world comes. It's a lot of fun for younger kids, however, featuring rides (all children like the miniature steam train), games (like the hay maze and hay jump), and performances (Josephine loves the incredibly silly puppet show). The U-pick pumpkin patch is also a regular (albeit muddy) stop for us.

Beyond The City Limits

Of course, most of the rides are in operation throughout the season without the additional cost.

The non-pumpkin U-pick strawberry fields are normally open in mid-June, and the raspberries tend to be ready in early July, although exact harvest times are weather dependent. You'll want to call first.

Snoqualmie Falls

6501 Railroad Ave. SE (Highway 202)
Snoqualmie

If you ever happened to catch an episode of the short-lived TV program "Twin Peaks," you will recognize this moody and awe-inspiring waterfall. Plummeting 268 feet, it is 100 feet higher than the Niagara Falls. This is one of the most popular tourist attractions in the state, drawing 1.5 million visitors each year. There are hiking trails throughout the area and the rustically elegant Salish Lodge stands ready to serve you breakfast, lunch or dinner, but it will cost you (reservations recommended).

Spring is when water volume is at its highest.

> **Snoqualmie Falls**
>
> Directions: From I-5 north or south, take I-90 exit (toward Spokane). Continue past Issaquah, take exit #27 and head toward Snoqualmie. Go north on Highway 202 and follow signs.

Hiking in the Cascades

Washington Trail Association
1305 Fourth Ave. Suite 512
Seattle, WA 98101-2401
(206) 625-1367
www.wta.org

In less than an hour by car, you can be on some of the best hiking trails on earth. Throughout the Cascade Mountains, you can find trails of all kinds and for all ability levels, complete with stunning views, solitude, and majesty. My best counsel is to contact the Washington Trail Association (see above). Their online hiking guide is excellent, as are their guidebooks.

If you're just looking for a little national forest getaway with the kids, however, one of our favorite "quickie" hikes is the Denny Creek trail which has the advantages of being a short drive, readily accessible from I-90, easy enough for even the youngest kids, and – obviously – close to a creek in which children can toss stones and dangle their feet. Although the total length of the trail is some 9 miles (ending at

> **Hiking in the Cascades**
>
> Directions to Denny Creek trail: From I-5 north or south, take I-90 exit (toward Spokane) and continue past Issaquah to exit #47. Turn left and pass under the freeway. Turn right at the "T" in the road and then onto Denny Creek Road. Drive about 3 miles to the Denny Creek campground, but just before getting there, turn left on the road (it has a sign) and continue to the parking lot.

Beyond The City Limits

Melakwa Lake), we tend to stick with the first mile, which more or less follows the creek and winds up at the base of a small waterfall/waterslide. The trail is well-maintained and not too steep. Take a picnic.

To hike on most of the trails in the Mount-Baker Snoqualmie National Forest, your family will need a Forest Pass ($5 for one day; $30 for the season). You can access an online, mail-in form at **www.fs.fed.us/r6/mbs/nwpass/order.htm** or you can purchase one at any ranger station, the Washington Trail Association, or at either REI or Metsker Maps (both of which are included in this book).

Skiing

Summit at Snoqualmie
Alpenhaus Lodge Gate Road 906
Snoqualmie
(206) 236-1600

Skiing

Cost: Adults $38 (full day), $32 half-day; youths $25 & $20; child $8.

Season/Hours: Mid-Fall through mid-Spring, depending on snow; hours vary, call first.

There are a dozen or so ski areas in the region, the closest being Summit at Snoqualmie (see below), although my sister (the biggest skier in the family, although not a parent) favors the Stevens Pass Ski Area (Skykomish – (206) 634-1645) and the Mt. Baker Ski Area (near the Canadian border – (360) 734-6771).

There's a lot to be said for proximity (45 minutes from downtown Seattle), however, and with the Summit at Snoqualmie offering four distinct areas – Alpental (expert), Summit West (snowboarding, bunny slopes), Summit East (less crowded), and Summit Central (intermediate) – there's something for everyone. Expect crowds, especially at Summit West. Our strategy is to rent our skis at REI (see pg. 54) and get to the slopes early.

Skate King

2301 140th Ave. NE
Bellevue
(425) 641-2046

This is probably the best all-around skating rink in the Seattle area. Call for schedule.

Skate King

Cost: Varies depending on time and type of session; skate rentals $1.50 - $4.

Hours: Wed.-Thurs, 4 p.m. - 11 p.m.; Fri., 7:30 p.m. - 11 p.m.; Sat., 10:30 a.m. - 10:30 p.m.: Sun. 1 p.m. - 8:30 p.m.; closed Mon.

Directions: From I-5 north or south, take the 520 bridge over Lake Washington. Take the 148th Ave. NE south exit and merge onto 148th Ave. NE. Turn right onto NE 24th St., then left onto 140th Ave. NE. It's located in the back of a shopping center so keep an eye out for the sign. Free parking in lot.

Beyond The City Limits

West by Ferry

If you just need to get out of the city, jump on a Washington State Ferry (Pier 50; 1-800-843-3779) and head to Bainbridge Island, Vashon Island, or Bremerton.

Things to Do

Bainbridge Island/Poulsbo

The trip is just 30-minutes, so it shouldn't surprise you to learn that most Seattleites think of it as a unique suburb, with many of the residents commuting daily to downtown via ferry.

The ferry lands you within walking distance of downtown Winslow, which has the charm of making you slow down to "island time" as you check out the shops along Winslow Way. When we are without our car, we generally take a hard left after leaving the dock, and stroll along the footpath and wander through **Waterfront Park**. The path ultimately loops up past the tennis courts and into a small playground. We then continue up to Winslow Way and poke our noses into various retailers, before ankling it into the laidback **Steamliner Diner** (397 Winslow Way – (206) 842-8595) for a good soup and sandwich lunch.

For those interested in further exploration, stop by the **Chamber of Commerce** visitor's center ((206) 842-3700) at the corner of Winslow Way and Highway 305 (straight ahead as you leave the ferry) for a "Trails Map" (there are some 10 trailheads on the island), a "Shoreline Interpretive Sites Map" (including 8 significant historical sites), or to ask about bed and breakfasts.

If you have the car, you might want to visit **Bloedel Reserve** (7571 NE Dolphin Dr. – continue straight off the ferry onto Hwy. 305 and follow it until you see Dolphin Dr. angling off to your right – (206) 842-7631). This is a beautiful, serene parcel of 80 acres, with lots for children to explore, including a Japanese garden, a reflection pool, and two miles of trails. Make sure to call at least a day in advance to reserve a spot (adults $6, children $4, under 5 are free).

Beyond The City Limits

Continue on Hwy. 305 to get to the cute, compact Scandinavian-infused port town of Poulsbo. Get here hungry and head straight for **Sluys Bakery** ((360) 697-2253) for heavy northern European breads and rich, buttery pastries. Carry your treats over to **Liberty Bay Park** (on the waterfront) or just wander around this tourist-friendly burg. The **Marine Science Center** ((360) 779-5549) is a fun, educational place where your little ones will get the opportunity to touch all sorts of "icky" things from the sea. Best of all, it's free. You also won't want to miss **Boehm's Chocolates** on Front Street ((360) 697-3318).

Vashon Island

A 15-minute ride on the passenger-only ferry from Colman Dock (the car ferry leaves from Fauntleroy in West Seattle) brings you to this diverse, bucolic island where bicycling and walking are popular (although you'll need to bring your own bike, as I am unaware of any rental places on the island).

The island is about 12 miles long and 8 miles across at its widest point, so unless you have small children, you really can do the entire island without a car (although a bike makes it easier), but you'll get some exercise, especially climbing/riding the sharp hill from the ferry.

There are antique shops, restaurants, and other retailers of browsing interest, but it's the natural, rural charm that brings people here. Vashon Island sports spectacular views of both Mt. Rainier and Mt. Baker and despite its small size, has a dozen parks for you to enjoy. The park closest to the ferry dock is the historic, 12-acre **Wingehaven Park** with undeveloped shoreline and beach access. The 43-acre **Paradise Ridge Park** offers fantastic equestrian (for information about riding and lessons call Cedar Valley Stables, (206) 463-9792) and walking trails. **Burton Acres-Jensen Point Park** is home to a swimming beach and boat launch from which to set out on kayaking or canoe explorations (for rental information call Vashon Island Kayak Co, (206) 463-9257).

Finally, if your kids have had enough bucolic, you might want to head to the **Burton Adventure Recreation Center**, which includes a skating "street course," a climbing gym, a 9-hole "disk" golf course, and BMX trails. Rentals are available for the skate park, but the rest of the equipment is strictly "bring your own." The skate park and climbing gym require entry fees, but the golf course and BMX are free. Call the Vashon Park District at (206) 463-9602 for hours and other details.

The social event of the season is the over 80-year-old **Strawberry Festival** which takes place in early July and includes a kooky, not-to-be-missed parade, entertainment of all sorts, crafts, food, dancing, and special children's activities.

Beyond The City Limits

Bremerton/Port Orchard

The longest of the ferry rides from downtown Seattle is the one-hour trip to Bremerton, home to the West Coast's largest naval shipyard, where the "mothball" fleet of decommissioned vessels haunts its harbor.

The **Bremerton Naval Museum** (130 Washington St., (360) 479-7447), located near the ferry terminal, is worth a look, featuring ship models, naval weapons, and all manner of memorabilia from the navy. Admission is free. Along the waterfront, you will find the destroyer USS *Turner Joy*, which in the summer is open for you to explore – also free.

Across Sinclair Inlet is the rustic town of **Port Orchard**, which you can reach by road (7 miles) or on the passenger-only ferry ((360) 876-2300). Its downtown features sidewalks covered with wooden arcades that keep you dry as you wander about the tourist-oriented area. Antiques abound.

To the North

As you drive north from Seattle, you will find urban sprawl at its worst, connecting Seattle to Everett with a continuous, mind-numbing repetition of housing developments and strip-centers. Almost every visitor to Seattle makes this journey, however, because this is the way to the vaunted Boeing factory tour, one of the single most popular attractions in the state.

Things to Do

Boeing Factory Tour

84th Street SW
Everett
(206) 544-1264 or 1-800-464-1476
www.boeing.com/companyoffices/aboutus/tours

There is nothing as unexpectedly exciting and memorable as a factory tour, and this is the Godzilla of all factory tours. This is where Boeing builds its wide-body aircraft, including the 767, 777, and the 747, the world's largest jets. In order to do this, they needed the world's largest building (by volume), which has grown to enclose some 472 million cubic feet, with a footprint of nearly 100 acres.

Boeing Factory Tour

Cost: Adults $5; children (under 15) $3; no children under 4'2" permitted (to reserve tickets, phone above numbers).

Tour times: Mon.-Fri., 9, 10, 11 a.m. and 1, 2, 3 p.m. (schedule subject to change; call 1-800-464-1476 for current times).

Directions: From I-5 north or south, take Exit 189 to State Highway 526 West. Drive for 3 to 3.5 miles and then follow the signs to the Tour Center. It is located near the west end of the assembly building.

Beyond The City Limits

You start with a video, then proceed to a balcony from which you can see all the stages of manufacturing. Finally, you are taken on a bus to Paine Field to watch the jets being tested on the runway. Wow! And I mean it.

Even the smallest kids will be fascinated by this slightly over one-hour tour, lead by a retired Boeing employee, although for safety reasons Boeing requires that children be at least 4 feet 2 inches tall. Even before September 11, security was tight. You may not take photos or videotape anywhere, and hand carried items (purses, backpacks, cameras, binoculars, cell phone, etc.) are not allowed. There are restrooms available before and after the tour, but none *during* the tour, so check with the kids prior to embarkation.

Everett AquaSox

Everett Memorial Stadium
3802 Broadway
(425) 258-3673
www.aquasox.org

Everett AquaSox

Cost: $6-10.

Schedule: Call for schedule.

Directions: From I-5 take exit 192 and follow the signs.

I love the Mariners, but this is a much better experience for small children. For one thing, the price to watch this Class A ball club is such that you don't mind if the kids get bored and want to leave early (which happens a lot at big league games). But the truth is that children simply don't get bored here.

How can they? There is a pig that carries extra baseballs out to the umpire; radio control dune buggy races between innings; children are called out onto the field to sing "Take Me Out to the Ballgame" during the 7th inning stretch; the silly frog mascot ("Webbly") is ever-present; in later innings, kids are given garbage bags to help out with clean-up. Promotions run the gamut from the inspiring to the goofy (like "Frogstock" when both the players and fans wear tie-die).

I think what we like best is that you come to watch baseball. The players come and go, but the fans remain the same and the result is a family-fun atmosphere that leaves you feeling like part of the team.

Personally, I like to buy the $10 seats behind home plate where friendly young servers make runs to the concession stand for you.

Beyond The City Limits

Edmonds

Edmonds is a beautiful little city on the shores of Puget Sound, with views of the Olympic Mountains and a small town feel. Mainly what you'll want to do is wander around the waterfront and downtown areas. The **Old Milltown** shopping center at 5th and Dayton has the look and feel of the old west, complete with boardwalks and covered arcades. The **Edmonds City Park** at 3rd and Howell Way has tons of playground equipment, a nature trail, and a wading pool. The waterfront is home to several popular parks as well.

Edmonds

Directions: From I-5 take Exit #177 (signage to Edmonds/Kingston Ferry). Follow Highway 104 West into Downtown Edmonds. On-street parking.

Heading South

Just south of Seattle along I-5, you will cut through Tukwilla, which is home to a huge concentration of big-box and discount stores, as well as the Southcenter indoor shopping mall. It's not as "sprawling" as the drive north, but you will pass through a dozen or so suburban cities between the city limits and Tacoma.

There are a lot of things for families in Tacoma and Pierce County – enough to fill a book of its own. Below you will find contact information for some of the major attractions:

Things to Do

Children's Museum of Tacoma

936 Broadway
Tacoma
(253) 627-6031

A fun place with dozens of hands-on activities, arts and crafts.

Children's Museum of Tacoma

Cost: Adults $3, children (3+) $4, under 3 are free; first Fri. of each month is free.

Hours: Tues.-Sat, 10 a.m. - 5 p.m.

The Tacoma Nature Center

1919 S Tyler St.
Tacoma
(253) 591-6439
www.tacomaparks.com

54-acre wetland habitat.

The Tacoma Nature Center

Cost: Free

Hours: Visitor's Center – Mon.-Fri., 8 a.m. - 5 pm.; Sat., 10 a.m. - 4 p.m.; closed Sun.

Preserve – Daily, 8 a.m.- dusk.

Beyond The City Limits

Northwest Trek

11610 Trek Drive East
Eatonville
(360) 832-6117
www.nwtrek.org

Northwest Trek

Cost: Adults $8.75; children (5-17) $6; tots (3-4) $4; under 3 free.

Season/Hours: April-Oct. Daily, 9:30 a.m. - closing times vary depending on season.

A 635-acre wildlife park, featuring a one-hour guided tram tour, where visitors can view herds of native animals such as bison, elk, moose, caribou, and mountain goats.

Point Defiance Park

N 54th at Pearl St.
Tacoma
(253) 305-1000
www.tacomaparks.com

Point Defiance Park

Cost: Free

Hours: Daily, dawn - dusk.

Point Defiance Zoo and Aquarium

Cost: Adults $7.75; children (4-13) $6; under 4 free.

Hours: Daily, 10 a.m. - 4 p.m. (open until 7 p.m. during summer months); closed Thanksgiving and Christmas.

Never Never Land Family Picnic Playground

Cost: Free

Hours: Daily, dawn - dusk.

Fort Nisqually Historic Site

Cost: Nominal

Hours: Wed.-Sun., 11 a.m. - 4 p.m. (open until 6 p.m. during summer months).

This nearly 700-acre park is the crown jewel of Tacoma's excellent park system. The park is home to several attractions:

Point Defiance Zoo and Aquarium
(253) 591-5337

This 29-acre zoo is large enough to offer an awesome array of animals yet small enough to let you get really close to them.

Never Never Land Family Picnic Playground
(253) 305-1000

Dozens of storybook character exhibits inhabit these picnic grounds.

Fort Nisqually Historic Site
(253) 591-5339

Tacoma Rainiers

2502 S Tyler St.
Tacoma
(253) 752-7707

Triple-A professional baseball.

Calendar

January-February:

Chinese and Vietnamese New Year
Celebrated in the International District with parade, dancers, fireworks.

Northwest Flower and Garden Show
Washington State Convention and Trade Center. (206) 789-5333

Festival Sundiata
Celebration of African cultures at Seattle Center. (206) 684-7200

March

Irish Week Festival
Seattle Center. (206) 684-7200

St. Patrick's Day Parade
Downtown. (206) 865-9134

Purim Carnival
Jewish holiday festival at the Jewish Community Center on Mercer Island. (206) 232-7115

Whirligig
Indoor rides and other entertainment for young children at Seattle Center. (206) 684-7200

April

Seattle Cherry Blossom and Japanese Cultural Festival
Seattle Center. (206) 684-7200

Skagit Valley Tulip Festival
Thousands of acres of blooming tulips, daffodils, and other flowers throughout the Skagit Valley as well as various family activities. 1-800-488-5477

Wild-n-Wooly Sheep Shearing
Sheep shearing festival at Kelsey Creek Farm in Bellevue. (425) 455-7688

Baseball Season Openers
The Seattle Mariners and Tacoma Rainiers start their seasons.

May

Opening Day of Boating Season
First Saturday of May. Boat parade through Montlake Cut at noon.

Northwest Folklife Festival
Nation's largest folk festival, featuring music, food, entertainment, and crafts at Seattle Center campus. (206) 684-7200

Calendar

Seattle International Children's Festival

Professional children's performers from around the world, including puppet shows, plays, music, dance. (206) 684-7338

Seattle Maritime Festival

A week of celebrating Seattle's Maritime heritage along the waterfront, including tugboat races. (206) 728-3410

University District Street Fair

Crafts, entertainment, food, and activities. (206) 547-4417

Pike Place Market Festival

Crafts, entertainment, food, and activities at Pike Place Market. (206) 682-7453

Poulsbo Viking Fest

Celebration of all things Scandinavian. (360) 779-FEST

June

Fremont Fair

Crafts, entertainment, food, activities, and the very popular Solstice Parade (watch out for naked cyclists!). (206) 633-4409

Everett AquaSox Baseball Opening Day

(425) 258-3673

July

Seafair

Four-week long, summertime celebration includes parades throughout the region, festivals, hydroplane races, the Navy's Blue Angels, the arrival of a U.S. Navy fleet, clowns, pirates, and dozens of other events and activities. For schedule: (206) 728-0123 or **www.seafair.com**.

Bite of Seattle

Food booths, entertainment, and family activities at Seattle Center. (206) 684-7200

Chinatown/International District Summer Festival

Arts & crafts, international food and entertainment, all reflecting the rich diversity of Seattle's International District. (206) 382-1197

Fireworks

Major fireworks displays over Elliott Bay and Lake Union. Smaller displays throughout the region.

Marymore Heritage Festival

Fourth of July weekend celebration of ethnic heritage at Marymore Park in Redmond. (206) 296-2964

Tivoli

Scandinavian heritage celebration at the Nordic Heritage Museum. (206) 789-5707

Pacific Northwest Arts and Crafts Fair

One of the nation's largest arts fairs, including a Kid's Fair, at Bellevue Square. (206) 454-4900

Wooden Boats Festival

Boat races, music, activities at the Center for Wooden Boats. (206) 382-BOAT

Kirkland SummerFest

(425) 822-7161

Vashon Island Strawberry Festival

A celebration of strawberries. Parade, food, crafts, entertainment, arts. (206) 463-6217

August

Taste of Edmonds

Performance, arts, crafts, food in downtown Edmonds. (425) 776-6711

Evergreen State Fair

Music, lumberjack show, stock car racing, rides, farm animals, etc. in Monroe. (425) 339-3309.

Bubble Festival

Bubble-related entertainment and activities at the Pacific Science Center. (206) 443-2001

Renton River Days

Entertainment, food, activities. (425) 430-6528

KOMO Kidsfair

Entertainment, rides, activities at Seattle Center. (206) 684-7200

Calendar

September

Bumbershoot
Labor Day weekend arts festival at Seattle Center, including entertainment, food, activities. (206) 281-8111 or **www.bumbershoot.org**.

The Puyallup Fair
(Western Washington State Fair)
Huge rural state fair in Puyallup with livestock, food, entertainment. (206) 841-5045

October

Kelsey Creek Farm Fair
Music, dancing, and "farm activities" at this hands-on farm/park. (425) 452-7254.

Issaquah Salmon Days
Celebration of the return of the salmon featuring a parade, entertainment, food, and children's activities in downtown Issaquah. (425) 392-0661

Northwest Bookfest
Everything books and authors, including children's activities such as puppet shows and the opportunity to write, illustrate, and bind their own books at the Washington State Convention Center. (206) 378-1883 or **www.nwbookfest.org**

November

Bon Marché Holiday Parade
Seattle's biggest holiday parade, taking place the day after Thanksgiving downtown. (206) 506-4FUN

Model Railroad Show
Displays, workshops and hands-on activities at the Pacific Science Center. (206) 443-2001

Yulefest
Scandinavian holiday celebration at the Nordic Heritage Museum. (206) 789-5707

Seattle Supersonics Basketball
season opener
The season begins. (206) 281-5800

Festival of Light
Celebration of winter holidays from various cultures. Seattle Center. (206) 441-1768

KING 5 Winterfest
Wintertime festival featuring ice skating, crafts, entertainment, and a beautifully lit International Fountain at Seattle Center. (206) 684-7200.

December

The Nutcracker Ballet
Pacific Northwest Ballet's performance of the classic holiday ballet, featuring costumes and sets by Maurice Sendak. (206) 441-2424

Chanukah Celebration
Games, candles, and activities at the Jewish Community Center on Mercer Island. (206) 232-7115

Christmas Ships
These brightly decorated ships cruise the area's waterways with carolers aboard. For a schedule of performances or to ride the Argosy Cruises ship: (206) 623-4252.

Index

Index

Index

Index

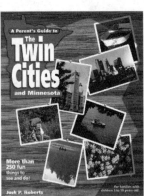

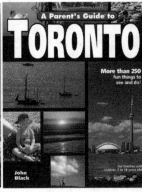